D0577865

Number Five: The Louise Lindsey Merrick Texas Environment Series

COASTAL TEXAS

Water, Land, and Wildlife

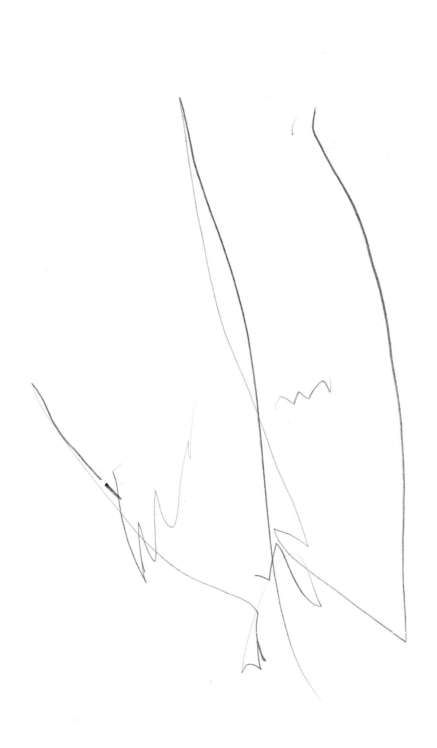

COASTAL TEXAS

Water, Land, and Wildlife

PHOTOGRAPHS AND TEXT

BY JOHN L. TVETEN

 TEXAS A&M UNIVERSITY PRESS *College Station*

Copyright © 1982 by John L. Tveten

All rights reserved

Library of Congress Cataloging in Publication Data

Tveten, John L.
    Coastal Texas.

    (The Louise Lindsey Merrick Texas environment
series; no. 5)
    1. Natural history—Texas.   2. Natural history—
Mexico, Gulf of.   I. Title.   II. Series.
QH105.T4T89   1982   508.764′1   82-40317
ISBN 0-89096-138-7

Manufactured in the United States of America
FIRST EDITION

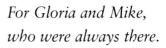

For Gloria and Mike,
who were always there.

Contents

Acknowledgments

I am indebted to many people who have assisted in the preparation of this labor of love. Many of the photographs and much of the information would not have been obtained without their help. The personnel of the following state and federal parks and refuges were always generous with their time and knowledge: Aransas National Wildlife Refuge, Laguna Atascosa National Wildlife Refuge, Padre Island National Seashore, Sea Rim State Park, Galveston Island State Park, and Goose Island State Recreation Area. Contributing, too, were the people at Armand Bayou Nature Center and Rick Tinnin of the University of Texas Marine Science Institute. A special thanks is due to manager Russ Clapper and the staff of Anahuac National Wildlife Refuge for their friendship and encouragement over many years.

Carl H. Aiken III and Dr. T. E. Pulley of the Houston Museum of Natural Science were companions on several trips along the Texas coast and provided a wealth of information and enjoyment. Captain Brownie Brown and his boat *Whooping Crane*; Sun Company, Inc., and Walter Erwin, who provided a helicopter ride over the Gulf; and David and Dorothy Lefkovits, with whom I visited the bird nesting islands in Galveston Bay, all played a vital role in obtaining photographs.

Finally, thanks to all the ardent birders, botanists, and friends and to my family, who shared many of the magic moments.

Preface

It was more than twenty-three years ago that I first saw the Texas coast, and I was immediately fascinated by its sand beaches, dunes, and teeming marshes. Part of this initial love may admittedly have been due to the fact that I fled a snowstorm farther north, but whatever the reason, I moved to coastal Texas shortly after the first visit and have remained there ever since.

With my family I have hiked long stretches of the beach and camped for many nights beside the Gulf of Mexico. I have collected seashells on those beaches and have birded intensively along the entire coast, from the Sabine to the Rio Grande.

This book is an attempt to depict the beauty and vitality of the coast, to portray the plants and animals that also call it home. The variety of wildlife there is truly astounding, and the ecological relationships are intricate beyond belief. This is not, however, a portfolio of underwater life, for I am not a diver, nor do the waters lend themselves to photography close to shore. It is, instead, a book about the world most people know—the beach they walk, the dunes they climb, the marsh they see but often fail to understand. There is no detailed treatment of the geology of the coastal plain or of the history associ-

ated with this most populous portion of the state. That would serve as a topic for dozens of other volumes much more extensive than this.

The economic aspects of the Texas coast—the production of oil and gas, shipping, agriculture, sprawling industrial complexes—are certainly important ones. They have an enormous impact on the natural history of the coast as well, for they ultimately compete for essential habitats and resources. Valuable estuaries have been drained and filled to provide waterfront living for a rapidly increasing population. Sand dunes have been flattened in the path of "progress." Pollution has taken its toll. We have too readily and too often compromised our natural resources for the sake of temporary financial gain. We have confused dominion over the land with domination of all it contains.

Yet in spite of the continued onslaught, a great deal remains to be seen and enjoyed, and that is the thrust of this book. Only by recognizing and understanding the balance of nature can we hope to preserve it. Only by appreciating the beauty around us can we conserve it for generations to come.

JOHN L. TVETEN

COASTAL TEXAS

Water, Land, and Wildlife

The Beach

A new day dawns in Texas as a red sun rises from the Gulf. Reflections sparkle and dance across the waves. Sandy beaches turn to flame.

There are many vistas in the state in which sunrise is an artistic masterpiece. One can but gasp with delight as the first rays touch the peaks of the Chisos, Davis, or Guadalupe mountains in the west. What more suitable frame for sunrise than palm trees along the Rio Grande or Ashe junipers and oaks on the limestone hillsides of the central portion of the state? Every dawn is special across the rolling Panhandle plains or among Big Thicket bogs and bayous.

In truth, the sun rises first on the bank of the Sabine River, for that boundary is farther east than the remainder of the curving, crescent Texas coast. Yet there is a special feeling to a sunrise on the beach. It seems to lay first claim to the magic of the morning; it must be very much like watching from the beginning of the earth.

Sometimes the sun ascends into a clear and crystal sky; sometimes into mists and fog that dim it to a ghostly glow. Clouds may spread across the east, catching color from the dawn and amplifying it manyfold. Or then again, that dawn may slip in cold and gray, no more than a subtle brightening of a leaden, storm-tossed sea.

On this coast there are no rugged seaside cliffs with breakers crashing on the rocks. There are no deep lagoons of sapphire blue, for this is a coastline of gently shelving sand. But no matter what the season, no matter what the weather of the moment, there are always adventures lying in wait. This edge of the Gulf of Mexico is a place of countless moods and constant charm, an endless symphony of sea and sand and surf.

Along the beach the birds await the dawn, some standing in the gentle surge with heads tucked sleepily beneath their wings. Gulls and terns seem everywhere, the ranks swelled in

Forster's and royal terns; laughing and ring-billed gulls

White pelicans

winter by their southward movement to escape snow and ice; some, however, remain throughout the year to constantly patrol the coast.

Gulls are, in general, larger than the terns with which they share status in the family Laridae. But the resident laughing gull and little Bonaparte's gull, which spends only the winter along the Texas shore, are smaller than the huge Caspian and royal terns.

Gulls have heavy, hooked beaks in contrast to the terns' sharp-pointed, dagger bills, and their tails are rounded rather than deeply forked. Both gulls and terns are graceful, buoyant fliers with long, slender wings.

Terns dive headfirst into the water in pursuit of small fish and other marine creatures on which they feed; gulls never dive, but rather hover above the surface or land to pick up morsels with their beaks. The gulls make up the beach's sanitation crew, devouring dead fish and invertebrates that wash ashore in great profusion.

Offshore in shallow water, or in the bays and channels that abound along the coast, white pelicans cruise like armadas of sailing ships, their considerable bulk belying their grace and beauty on the wing. Like the gulls and terns, pelicans are most common in the wintertime. In summer they fan out across the western portion of the continent to breed in inland lakes, some ranging northward far into Canada. One small colony remains to nest in the Laguna Madre, the shallow body of water between Padre Island and the Texas mainland.

It is its beak, of course, for which the pelican is famous—a beak that, in the well-known verse of Dixon Merritt, "holds more than his belican." With this formidable appendage the white pelican scoops up fish, often working in cooperation with others of its species to herd schools of fish into shallow water where they are easier to surround and catch. Unlike the brown pelican, the only other member of the family to be found in North America, the white pelican does not

Dowitchers

Long-billed curlew

dive to capture fish. The brown pelican plunges headlong into the water from heights of as much as thirty feet, but his white relatives are content to swim or wade and dip up prey in their ballooning beaks.

Indeed, it is the structure of a bird's beak that perhaps reveals most about its habits and familial relationships. Bill shape is the key to feeding behavior, and on such traits are taxonomic boundaries drawn.

Hordes of shorebirds throng the beaches and mud flats of the Texas coast in confusing array. Three dozen species seem almost too complex to comprehend, yet they may be categorized by the shape and function of their bills.

Chunky little plovers scamper about, picking up small worms, crustaceans, and mollusks with their short, dovelike beaks. Sandpipers probe the sand with longer, slimmer bills for the same food items.

Dowitchers stitch their way across the mud flats like miniature sewing machines, bobbing constantly up and down as they drive their beaks into the soft bottom in search of burrowing animals. In the surf they proceed more slowly but with equal dedication, frequently with heads submerged as waves wash over them. These and the other sandpipers tend to segregate somewhat by size, for those species with longer legs and bills are capable of feeding at a greater depth.

Largest and most striking of the sandpipers found along the coast is certainly the long-billed curlew. The decurved bill reaches a length of seven inches and is used for extracting crabs and worms from deep within their winding burrows. Not exclusively a beach-front bird, and equally at home catching insects among the grasses, the curlew is also found on prairies and rangelands across the West.

There are many variations on the theme. The American oystercatcher has a laterally compressed, chisellike bill with which it pries open shells of oysters, clams, and other bivalves in order to extract a meal. The avocet possesses a long, thin bill with an upward curve, one of the few with such a strange configuration. It feeds by sweeping its bill from side to side along the bottom, picking up the small invertebrates it chances to disturb. On the beach and jetties, the ruddy turnstone darts about, turning over shells and rocks and catching tiny creatures thus exposed. Its beak, too, is uniquely shaped, sharply pointed and turned slightly upward at the tip.

Just as each plover or sandpiper has its own specific niche to fill, so does every other bird as well. They are almost always in view, the most visible of the many life forms with which the beach abounds. Some are colorful and readily recognized; some seem hopelessly alike in shades of tan and gray.

Herons of a half-dozen species, including the towering great blue heron, the smaller little blue and Louisiana herons, and the immaculately plumaged snowy and great egrets, stalk the shallows. Each feeds up to its own depth, depending on its stature. Unique among them is the reddish egret, a species that in the United States is confined to southern Florida and the Texas coast, for it has a feeding behavior all its own. Spreading its wings, and with shaggy head and neck plumes in disarray, it prances and kicks and lurches about, looking for all the world like a disheveled derelict in a drunken dance. The behavior is called "canopy feeding," and the extended wings cast shadows on the water and make it easier to see beneath the surface glare. Fish or crustaceans seek shelter in those shadows too, unaware that a spear is poised and waiting just above.

It is apparent that the birds exert a major influence on the other creatures of the beach. They are at the top of many of the myriad food chains, preying on other living organisms and scavenging the dead. It is an important role to play, a role they do not accept by choice but rather inherit by the very fact that they are birds. It is simply in their nature to do the things they do. And this they accomplish with style and grace, with beauty of both hue and form.

Willet

Willet

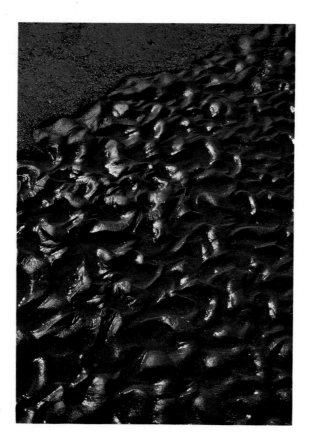 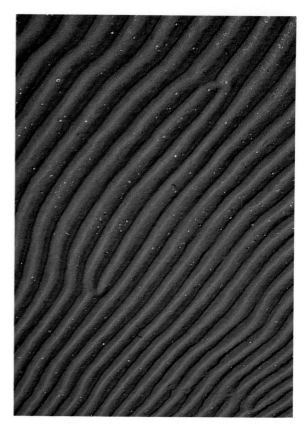

The beauty and variety of the beach is seen in other aspects of its long and sinuous sweep. Nearly four hundred miles of Texas coastline borders on the Gulf, much of it in the form of barrier islands separated from the mainland by shallow bays. Rivers bring down their sediments from across the state, and channels and inlets allow interchange between the bays and the open Gulf. There is a never-ending sense of change. Waves wash away some segments of the beach and drop their burden to rebuild it somewhere else. Persistent tides lap against the sand to etch their image, while frothy waves roll in to leave mosaics made of iridescent foam. Birds weave a tapestry of tracks, as do the mollusks and the crabs. The composite is a work of art, but its beauty is at best a transitory one, for bubbles burst and new tides erase the printed patterns, later to replace them with others of their own.

Creatures of the sandy beach are faced with the hazards of life in this zone of tides and surf, constantly pulled and buffeted by the waves, alternately exposed and awash in the ebb and flow. To escape these forces, many burrow into the sand. Some remain continually unseen beneath the surface; others emerge at times to move about and search for food.

Predators of all sizes stalk the water's edge. Some crabs and snails, like the birds, feed on others of their kind. The crabs have crushing claws to use; the snails employ a variety of other means to subdue their prey. The lettered olive, with its lovely polished shell, slides along on a large, muscular foot, engulfing small clams and consuming them. The moon snail, or shark's eye, uses its radula, a ribbonlike band covered with tiny teeth, to rasp away at another shell until it drills a small hole through which it eats the occupant. Many empty shells strewn on the beach bear the telltale round hole of this fascinating carnivore.

There are grazers—sea urchins and other snails and crabs—that feed on algae, and there are the scavengers that find decaying matter in

Gull tracks

Blue crab

Striped hermit crab

Sea anemones

the surf. There are countless filter-feeders—oysters and mussels, sponges, worms, and barnacles—that live by straining microscopic plankton from the sea. Each uses the mechanism it has inherited, and all are successful in their own ways.

Roughly one hundred species of crabs are found along the Texas coast. Some range the shoreline and mud flats; some are found in the deeper waters of the Gulf. A few, called commensal crabs, are so specialized that they live only within the shells of specific mollusks, an ecological niche only they are adapted to fill. Hermit crabs of several kinds have no tough carapace or shell with which to protect themselves. Thus they use empty snail shells, appropriating them as their own. As they grow, they periodically trade their borrowed refuges for larger ones.

Some crabs are extremely colorful, while others are the epitome of camouflage techniques. Best known, certainly, is the edible blue crab, on which a major commercial fishery is based. Able to tolerate a wide range of conditions, it is found in the open Gulf as well as in the bays and in marshes and ponds of very low salinity.

Among the rocks of the jetties are sea anemones that do, indeed, look more like many-petaled flowers than the carnivorous animals they really are. The petallike tentacles, however, are armed with stinging cells called nematocysts that inject venom through long, barbed filaments when disturbed. With these weapons the anemones paralyze their prey, the tentacles then drawing it into the waiting mouth. Exposed by low tide, anemones no longer look the part of shimmering flowers. Instead, they fold their tentacles into themselves and take on a formless disguise, sometimes acquiring a covering of sand and shell fragments as further camouflage and protection from the dessicating sun and scouring, wave-carried sand.

Abundant everywhere on the sandy beach are seashells of great variety. Most are empty,

Small beach-drift bivalve shells

lifeless, yet lovely husks of mollusks large and small. Hundreds of species have been identified along the Texas coast. Many represent the Carolinian province, spreading across the Gulf of Mexico from the lower Atlantic Coast. There is also a Caribbean influence, however, especially along the southern reaches of the crescent. Most frequently encountered are the bivalves, or pelecypods, the clams and clamlike animals that include the oysters, arks, mussels, scallops, lucinas, cockles, tellins, and other families and genera with less familiar names. Many live buried in the sand or mud; others, like the scallops, can swim about by rapidly opening and closing their shells. Some burrow into timbers and pilings or even into solid rock. All are filter feeders; that is, they take in water through one siphon tube, filter out the plankton and detritus on which they feed, and expel the water through another tube.

The bivalves may at first seem very much alike, but each has its own distinctive struc-ture and unique charm. Tiny coquinas, *Donax*, that inhabit the surf-zone sands in great profusion have sunrise rays of purple, rose, blue, or yellow. Delicate butterfly tellins blush rosy pink, while giant cockles are varnished with mahogany and rust. Fragile angel wings are easily broken by the waves upon the sand, yet sturdy, sculptured arks of several species survive intact in even the most tempestuous of seas, still covered by the dark and mossy protein growth called the periostracum.

More varied in appearance are the gastropods, or snails. They too, of course, vary greatly in size, some reaching nearly a foot in length while others remain no larger than a grain of rice. The gastropods, whose name means "stomach-footed," crawl freely about on that muscular foot and are far more mobile than their bivalve relatives.

Most snail shells are beautifully spiraled works of calcareous art, each starting with a tiny whorl and enlarging as the snail grows. Each animal secretes from its mantle the cal-

Rock shells

cium carbonate to build its protective home and adorns it with sculpture and pattern according to some instinctive blueprint that is innate within its species.

Large whelks, *Busycon*; rock shells, *Thais*; and moon snails, *Polinices*, wash in great quantities upon the sandy beach. Olives, murexes, and tulip shells are found in lesser numbers, as are pretty species with such fanciful names as Scotch bonnet, sundial, and baby's ear. The delicate wentletraps, little spiral staircases of gleaming white, are among the most exquisite of the shells found along the Texas shore.

Each has its own environmental niche to fill, its own habitat and habits as dictated by its molluskan personality. On the jetties are limpets holding tightly to the rocks and tiny periwinkles, *Littorina*, that seem somehow too small and fragile to withstand the constant pounding of the surf. Both feed by grazing on the algal growths that coat the rocks with greenish threads. Here are found the rock shells, too, but they are carnivores at

heart. Sometimes called oyster drills, they use their rasping radulae to feed on barnacles, oysters, and other bivalves that are anchored to the rocks or reefs.

How different is the behavior of the purple sea snails, several different species of *Janthina*, which are pelagic animals. Buoyed by rafts of bubbles trapped in mucus, they float about on the trackless sea, feeding on the much larger jellyfishes, the stinging Portuguese men-of-war. Only when driven ashore by strong southeasterly winds in spring are they found with any frequency upon the beach.

Other mollusk classes include, in much smaller numbers, the scaphopods, or tusks, with their inch-long, cylindrical shells, and the chitons girdled in armor plates. Most highly developed of the phylum are the cephalopods, including the octopus and squid.

Variety is the essence of the beach, a variety reflected in both the diversity of its inhabi-

Laughing gull

tants and the complexity of its many moods. Each sunrise is different from the ones that have come before. Every day, every hour, brings a new experience.

The ubiquitous coastal birds, for example, present a state of nearly constant change. Populations wax and wane, moving with the seasons in response to instinctive drives that serve to push them on. Even birds that remain throughout the year may undergo marked changes as a result of their own internal clocks.

The head feathers of both sexes of the resident laughing gull turn black in breeding plumage, a transformation that occurs in early spring. Hormonal stimuli cause their bills and legs to turn a deep blood red as well. After the nesting season, another molt takes place, and the black again gives way to white feathers marked with dingy gray.

The same is true for many other species throughout the avian world. Loons and grebes that only winter in these southern waters are hardly recognizable as the same birds that breed much farther north. Colorful patterns of spring and summer have been replaced by somber hues, and characteristic calls are silenced, for there are no territories to proclaim. The many shorebird species are all much more alike in plumage here than they are upon their Arctic nesting grounds. Ducks of fall and early winter are frequently drab and difficult to tell apart, for drakes undergo a postnuptial molt to an "eclipse" plumage similar to that displayed by their less colorful mates.

Not all individuals, however, are in biological agreement about the time for change. Some rush the season; others are slow to respond. Thus, varied plumage patterns occur throughout the periods of molt. In late winter, some laughing gulls may already have attained their black hoods, while others show little evidence of the approaching spring. Added to the confusion of seasonal and sexual differences is the fact that young birds are often quite unlike their parents. Gulls may take several years to mature, going through a series of molts in which they are mottled grayish brown with dark or banded tails, gaining only gradually the immaculate feathering of the adults. All mass together, presenting a challenge in identification but adding constant and dynamic beauty to the beach.

With the lengthening daylight hours of spring, many birds begin their grueling migration northward, to be replaced in part by others coming from still farther south. In the fall, the flow will be reversed, and huge flocks will again descend to spend the winter along the Gulf of Mexico. Indeed, more bird species may be observed on the Texas coast than in any other place in North America. Christmas bird counts here annually rank at or near the top; migrations attract bird watchers from around the world.

The birds are primarily species of the eastern portion of the country, but there are strong influences from the West as well, especially along the lower coast. Species of the far North reach Texas with the aid of winter storms, and tropical ones from the Caribbean may appear in the wake of hurricanes and storms from the sea. Others cross the Rio Grande from Mexico. The possibilities number well above four hundred.

Most birds seen along the beach are, of course, the water birds: loons, grebes, pelicans, cormorants, ducks, herons, plovers and sandpipers, gulls, and terns. Because they inhabit open areas and frequently make long flights while exposed to the uncertainties of weather at sea, they are much more likely to be blown far off course. They may also join a flock made up of related birds of yet another species and be led astray, so to speak, and far from their normal range. Thus it is that rare ducks, gulls, or shorebirds from far-off regions are more likely to turn up on the Texas coast than are other birds that spend sedentary lives tucked away inland in some sheltered niche.

During spring migration, however, small land birds may also congregate along the shore. Moving northward from their winter homes in Mexico or Central and South America, orioles, grosbeaks, buntings, vireos, flycatchers, thrushes, and warblers funnel up the

Male redhead ducks

Yucatan Peninsula and from there fly nonstop across the Gulf of Mexico. Even the tiny ruby-throated hummingbird makes such a monumental flight each year.

Leaving Yucatan at dusk and flying throughout the night, they ordinarily reach the Texas coast the next day. Pushed by the prevailing southeasterly winds, they have little trouble. They may cross the coastline at an altitude of a thousand feet or more and disperse across the eastern portion of the state. Some land to rest and feed in yards and gardens of cities near the Gulf; others continue on into the forests of deep East Texas before they stop for a brief respite.

Even during the peak of the migration season, from late March through early May, if there are blue skies and warm breezes there may be no buildup of birds along the coast. They are spread out thinly along the entire flyway. If, however, the trans-Gulf migrants encounter less than favorable weather, their lives are immediately placed in peril. Bucking strong northerly headwinds or flying into a chilling rain, they lose altitude and fly just above the surface of the water, perhaps even stopping to rest on boats or offshore platforms in their path. Many do not make it, and they may one day be washed up on the shore.

Those that do survive stop to rest as soon as they make landfall on the beach. They perch in the grasses of the dunes and marshes. Some land upon the sand and hop to cover, too tired to fly the remaining few yards. Each shrub and tree is a haven for the exhausted birds.

It is at times like this—after rainstorms and cold fronts have pushed across the coast— that oak mottes and seaside groves of salt-cedars, or tamarisks, are alive with the most colorful of birds. Tiny warblers of thirty species, many garbed in brilliant yellow, flit about the branches, gleaning insects and refueling for the continuation of their flight. There are blue and rose-breasted grosbeaks,

Immature black-legged kittiwake

indigo buntings, scarlet tanagers, and brilliant orange northern orioles. Brightest of all is the male painted bunting with its red breast, blue head, and lime green back. *Mariposa pintada*, the early Spanish settlers called it, "painted butterfly." To the French it was the *nonpareil*, "without equal," a name still widely in use throughout the South. It may remain to nest, with its plain green mate, in brushy thickets not too far inland from the coast.

These, of course, are not normally coastal birds, yet they do occur in season to add additional excitement to the scene. During the remainder of the year the typical shore and water birds hold sway, supplemented by occasional exotic species prone to wander across the Gulf.

The birds are not the only creatures that move or migrate along the beach. In fall the monarch butterflies head south, destined for their recently discovered winter home in the mountain forests of Mexico. By the dozens,

indeed by the hundreds and even thousands, they come from the midsection of the continent where they have undergone their near-magic metamorphosis during the final days of summer. Reaching the water's edge, some strike out across the Gulf, but most follow the curving sweep of sand and surf.

They flutter past on wings that somehow seem too fragile to withstand exposure to the wind and spray. At night they rest with folded wings among tall grasses or spikes of goldenrod beside the beach. They cling to the lacy branches and leaves of tamarisks like orange flowers hung in pendant clusters. And in the morning, warmed by the sun until their flight muscles can function once again, they resume the journey that may ultimately carry them two thousand miles.

In spring those same overwintering monarchs turn around and head back north, this time flying less purposefully, for they will never make it all the way. Many stop in Texas to lay their eggs and, the design fulfilled, to

Migrating monarch butterflies on tamarisk

Young spiders on driftwood

die. From those eggs, through milkweed-eating caterpillars and dormant pupae to adults, other butterflies resume the flight. The process repeated quickly through several generations, monarchs finally return to the northern portions of their range. Then, instinctively, the last generation will turn once more and strike out for Mexico, to seek a forest it has never seen but whose location is "known" through heredity.

There are many such stories, though perhaps few so dramatic, acted out upon the sand. Ladybugs and other beetles also move along the coast, as do other insects less well known. Spiders hatch from egg cases placed on driftwood logs or among beachside grasses and debris, and they disperse by ballooning on strands of silk spun to catch the onshore breeze. Beneath the waves the swimmers also move about. The fishes, crabs and shrimp, jellyfish and other small invertebrates—even the mammalian bottlenose dophin, the common cetacean species of the coast—move

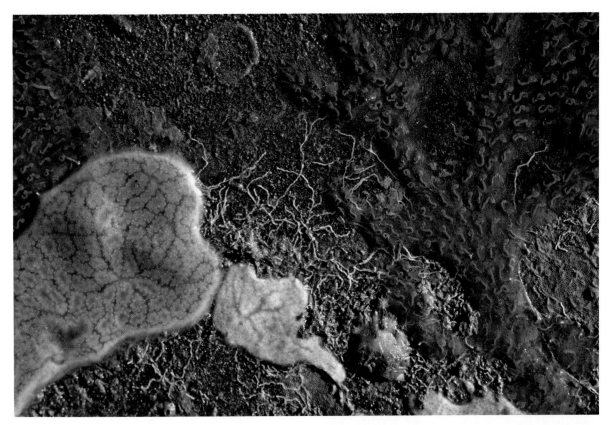

Colonial tunicates

with the currents or migrate in and out of shallow water according to the seasons and their stages of development.

Other residents of the coastal waters are much less mobile within their chosen habitats. Some burrow deeply into the bottom sediments, while others lie quiescent on the sand. Many are found primarily on the jetties and rock groins constructed to protect ship channels and reduce sand movement along the beach. Because of the nature of the Texas coast, the man-made jetties and groins are the only rocky habitats available, and they have their own attendant floral and faunal populations.

Attached to many of the submerged rocks are encrusting sponges, the most primitive of the multicellular animals. They have no true organs or organ systems and subsist on oxygen and planktonic food absorbed from the water that passes through their body openings. There are relatively few species of sponges in the northwestern Gulf of Mexico as compared to the eastern Gulf off Florida,

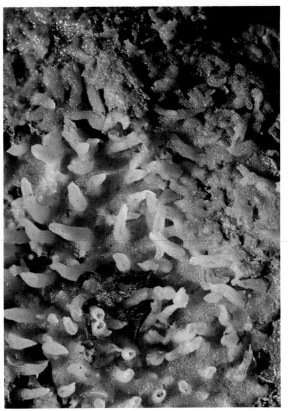

Sponge and brittle star

probably because of a combination of cool winters, sandy water, and lack of suitable substrates on which to live. Sponges are highly variable in appearance and difficult to identify, speciation depending largely on microscopic examination of the glassy or limy spicules that make up their skeletons.

Starfish and brittle stars can also be found among the rocks, as can the spiny sea urchins that feed on the seaweeds growing there. Isopods and amphipods—small crustaceans such as the sea roach and beach flea—leap and scurry about, and crabs of several kinds hide within the crevices. Many of these life forms are most abundant on the jetties along the southern section of the coast, where the warmer waters permit greater biological diversity.

Many creatures of the sea are, upon hatching, free-swimming larvae that later mature and settle down to a sedentary life. They bear little physical resemblance to the adults, and they make up the great mass of plankton that forms the basis for many of the oceanic food

chains. Crabs begin life as almost unrecognizable larval forms, as do the acorn barnacles that will eventually grow cemented to the rocks.

Strangest of all, perhaps, and certainly among the most poorly understood, are animals called tunicates. They are classified in the same scientific phylum, Chordata, as are the fish, birds, mammals, and other bony animals, for the minuscule larvae possess within their tails supporting rods called notochords. At this stage they look somewhat like tiny tadpoles, but they later lose the notochord and cease to move about, never developing the vertebrae that distinguish their closest relatives. Some, like the sea squirts, are solitary as adults, while others cluster in multicolored jellylike or rubbery masses on the surface of the rocks.

Frequent storms add interest to a walk along the beach. Shorebirds huddle against the wind, and gulls sail on rigid wings above the gray and churning waves. There is a feel-

Red knots

Laughing gull

Portuguese man-of-war

Cabbagehead jellyfish

Southern stingray

Sargassum nudibranch

ing of remoteness and a sense of great discovery, for it is then that the Gulf gives up its secrets and they are washed up on the sand.

There are fish of many shapes and sizes, some of species seldom seen—streamlined sharks and flat stingrays, red snapper, menhaden, barred sheepsheads, and strange lookdowns of shimmering silver. The harmless cabbagehead jellyfish washes ashore with enormous numbers of its fellows, as does the venomous Portuguese man-of-war, *Physalia physalis*. The latter has a purple, gas-filled float beneath which trail tentacles armed with stinging nematocysts. Long after it seems dead and dried upon the beach, the stinging cells can still inflict a painful wound.

Physalia, in spite of outward appearances, is not a single animal, but rather a colony of many smaller ones. Sometimes called "zooids" or "persons," the individual polyps are of many different types, each adapted to perform a special function for the whole. Some form

the float; others, the tentacles and mouth parts. It is a complex system that is difficult to comprehend.

Most common of the seaweeds to be tossed up on the beach is sargassum weed, or gulfweed. It is a pelagic plant, floating free on the open sea, buoyed by small air bladders and subject to the whims of the currents and the winds.

Like most of the other plants called "seaweeds," sargassum is a marine alga, distantly related to the giant kelp, which does not occur in the northwestern Gulf. Both are brown algae, and there are numerous species of both green and red algae along the Texas coast as well. Some are slender, bright green filaments, while others are leafy, branching, or crustose growths.

Sargassum brings with it a unique array of animals, its own attendant zoo that drifts with it across the surface of the water. The sargassum nudibranch, a shell-less gastropod,

Monarch butterfly

Sheepshead

is found nowhere else but in association with its host. Leafy lobes along its sides and near-perfect protective coloration make it almost impossible to detect as it creeps and swims among the fronds. Similar camouflage protects the frilly sargassumfish and the sargassum crabs and shrimp. Pipefish, flatworms, anemones, hydroids, and bryozoans also share the microcosm. All are adapted to a life solely on sargassum weed.

Most creatures that are found upon the sand have lived out their lives but perhaps leave behind their progeny, whose task it is to carry on. Winds and waves both take their toll, as do the countless predators. It is an endless cycle that eventually claims the fish of the sea and the birds and butterflies of the air. Each storm must end, however, and the plants and animals go on about the only life they know. And no predator takes all the prey.

The system has functioned for untold millions of years, adapting and changing when faced with the necessity. The beach bears wit-

Pleistocene-fossil horse tooth

ness to these changes, too, for here can be found evidence of creatures long since extinct.

Pleistocene fossils wash from the clays underlying the more modern sands along the upper coast. Lying on the beach with recent shells are mammal bones and turtle shell. Teeth from prehistoric horses, camels, and bison are frequently found, as are fragments of deer antlers and sloth claws. Half buried in the sand may be a massive mammoth tooth.

A million years from now, things will certainly have changed some more. Animals that are living now may well be fossils, too. The sands may be washed away or buried beneath sediments of newer age. But for the present, the beach remains a fascinating stretch of sand, whether reddened by an April dawn or bathed in the glow of the autumn moon.

Behind the beach rise dunes of drifting sand, dazzlingly bright in the subtropic sun. Although dunes are found along much of the Texas coast, they are most majestic on the southern barrier islands. On Mustang and Padre islands they are capped by sea oats, a tall grass that sways in the warm Gulf breeze or is whipped by fierce hurricane winds.

The light-colored sand grains, rounded in shape with frosted surfaces, are carved and etched by countless collisions as they are driven before the wind. Most are of quartz from the weathering away of the granitic rocks that make up a major portion of the earth's surface. Here too, however, are pink grains of feldspar, bits of limestone from previous oceans, and darker grains of basalts and other rocks that trace their ancestry to an age of vulcanism. Fragments of shell, weathered past all identity, make their contribution to the dunes as well.

We can but imagine the history of these grains of sand. Once plucked as boulders from sheer mountain cliffs by freezing ice and snow, washed from eroding prairies, or driven by desert winds, they have been carried by streams and rivers toward the sea, becoming ever smaller on their way. Some are of an age beyond human comprehension; some are young as measured against the scale of geologic time.

Once in the sea, the sands are again moved shoreward by relentless waves that drift and tumble them along unseen beneath the surface. As each wave washes upon the beach, it brings with it the burden that it carries, leaving some grains but reclaiming others as it retreats.

In succession, each wave picks up the sand, moves it forward, and puts it down again. Each of these movements may be small, but there is no need for haste. Time means little to the sea. Thousands of waves break upon the beach each day.

Winter storms or summer hurricanes may for a time reverse this trend. With greater energy, huge waves pick up the sand and wash it out to sea. There it will remain, deposited

near shore, until the storm subsides and smaller waves again begin their rebuilding task.

No individual grain of sand remains in one place for long. The change may not be obvious, however, for there are others to take its place. And just as each grain of sand may move, so may the beach itself. It is not an immovable object in the face of the sea's irresistible force. There will always be a beach, at least in a time frame possible to comprehend, but it may move inland or seaward many times in the centuries to come.

Once ashore, the sand is subject to the whims of the wind. As it dries, it is blown inland by the prevailing onshore breeze. It swirls and tumbles along, stratifying by mass as the lighter particles are swept away.

At the upper reaches of the beach, dunes begin to form. They, in turn, trap still more sand. The mounds grow higher. Banners of sand blow from their crowns, and slipfaces flow like rivers down their flanks. They seem alive—growing, shrinking, moving on.

Seen in the low-angle light of dawn or dusk, the dunes are a fairyland of shadows and contrasts. At midday the sands are glistening white; now they take on richer hues. Wind ripples pattern the surface like that of a solid sea. Strange, sensual shapes build where breezes drop their crystal cargo as they swirl.

There is a sameness to the dunes, yet there is remarkable variety as well. Their essence is movement, change, a restless wanderlust that seems to lead them on.

Only when covered by vegetation do the sands become stable and the dunes cease to move. Vining plants trail across the dunes, rooting successively at the nodes and forming a network that holds this mercurial world in place. It is not a hospitable environment in which to grow, for blowing sand grains scour the leaves, and water sinks quickly away. Salt-laden winds stunt and dehydrate all but the hardiest of plants.

This is, in effect, a desert habitat—albeit a desert within sight of the sea—and many of the plants exhibit traits like those of their in-

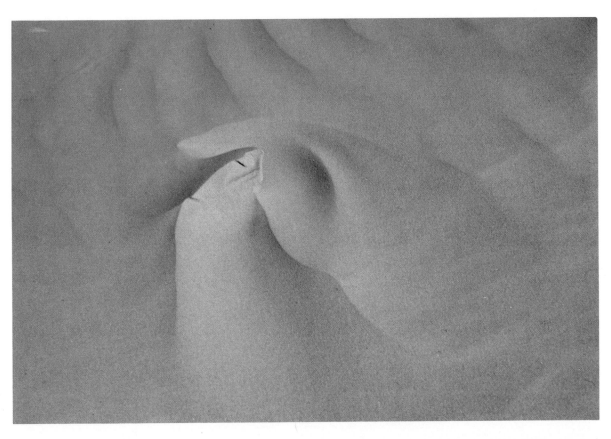

Beach morning-glory

Sunflowers

land desert kin. Leaves are thick and succulent, densely hairy, or reduced in size, all adaptations to decrease water loss to the air by transpiration and to protect the leaves from the ravages of sun and sand. Stems are tough and wiry, and roots grow deeply into the porous soil in search of precious moisture.

Except for the tall, stately sea oats and some of the other resilient grasses, most of the plants grow low to the ground, hugging it to blunt the forces of the winds.

The first colonizing plants are faced with an epic struggle. Partially covered by the shifting dunes, they spread by off-shoots and runners, emerging again as if gasping for breath in the enveloping sea of sand. Buried leaves quickly die, but others form to trap the brilliance of the sun and produce food energy for further bursts of growth. Even in death they add organic nutrients to the soil.

In the shelter of those first pioneers, and with the sustenance they provide, other plants take root and grow. They, in turn, trap still more seeds carried by the swirling winds. Animals find cover here, and they, too, serve as vectors for seed dispersal. A stable plant community is born.

So great are the modifications for this environment that many of these specialized plants grow nowhere else. They are no longer capable of life in the shade or in rich, heavy soil. Inexorable changes, adaptations for survival, have created unique species of the dunes.

White-flowered beach morning-glory and rich magenta goat's-foot morning-glory are two of the prettiest and most important of the sand-dune plants. Both have succulent, bright green leaves and long, interlacing runners that also give the latter the common name of railroad vine. This is their station in life; they inhabit only the coastal sands.

Morning-glories characteristically open their blooms at night and reach full beauty in the early light of dawn. Touched by the harsh, glaring sun reflecting from the sand, they

Goat's-foot morning-glory

Beach morning-glory

close and wilt away. Some will have been fertilized by passing insects and form seeds within thickening ovaries, but this genesis is less vital for continued existence in plants that also reproduce by vegetative growth.

So, too, does the beach evening-primrose shrink from the noonday sun. The large yellow flowers are thin-petaled and delicate, unable to withstand strong light or heat. Not so the leaves, however, for they are cloaked in fine, grayish hairs that provide shade and protection for the tender cells beneath. Many other species in this plant community share the same adaptations.

Common to the dunes are several kinds of crotons, called dove-weeds and goatweeds, with their distinctive ovate, silvery leaves. Their identification is difficult at best, for all appear much the same to the untrained eye.

Partridge pea and whitestem wild-indigo dot the sands of the southern barrier islands. Ground-cherry, ragweed, phlox, and wild mustards add their stabilizing influence, as do the round-leafed pennyworts, or *Hydrocotyls*,

Beach evening-primrose

Downy, or silverleaf, sunflower

Sea-purslane

Padre Island live oaks

that sprout like miniature parasols from a network of spreading roots and runners.

In low spots between the dunes or along regions more often flooded by storms and tides grow sea-purslane and *Salicornia,* or pickleweed, with its tart, vinegary taste. Both have thick, fleshy leaves or stems that store moisture against the broiling sun.

The botanical catalog is lengthy and varied. Species differ for different sections of the coast, and floral displays change with the season. As is the case in almost every habitat across the continent, however, the composites are always on display. They are hard to identify, for the many species are similar in form, mostly yellow or white, and different mainly in the finer botanical details of the flower heads. They are called composites because what at first appears to be a single flower proves, on close examination, to be a cluster of tiny blooms, each subservient to the whole. Petallike elements are called ray flowers; those in the central disk, disk flowers. Some, like the

thistles, have only disk flowers. A few have only ray flowers.

Prominent members of the profuse composite family are the sunflowers, the gaillardias, and dozens of species called, with varying degrees of accuracy, "daisies." Most species found along the coast have tough, almost spiny leaves or are typically covered with hairs. The downy sunflower has a luxuriant sheltering coat of long, white hairs, particularly on the tender new growth.

Few trees grow on the dunes themselves, although such species as hackberry, live oak, red bay, and yaupon holly colonize the coastal sands of more sheltered areas behind the dunes and saline marsh.

Striking for their bowed yet strangely graceful shapes, however, are a half-dozen live oaks on the drifting sands of Padre Island, remnants of a forest that once covered portions of that longest of the Texas barrier islands. Their twisted, sculptured forms are due both to constant pressure of the prevailing winds and to

the salt-laden ocean spray that prunes the branches by stunting their outward growth to windward.

Grasses of many species are the most abundant stabilizing plants. Half buried, they spread slowly but persistently, trapping wind-blown grains of sand to facilitate further dune formation. The first sprig of grass, however small, along the upper beach breaks the flow of air, and in the swirling eddy the sand begins to build. The grass continues to grow. More sand is added. With infinite patience, grain by grain, nature builds a monument.

If undisturbed, the ridge of dunes, the fore-dunes, above the beach becomes well covered by its mat of grass. Sea oats, bitter panicum, gulfdune paspalum, dropseeds, and others blanket the surface.

Inland, the deep sands lie more evenly in repose, building only low ridges and hummocks with marshy areas between. Here there is more moisture, and the diversity of plants is greater still. Grass species of the higher dunes share the habitat with marsh-hay cordgrass, bushy bluestem, seashore saltgrass, red love-grass, and dozens of others in apparent botanical confusion. Each species has its own environmental niche to fill, yet the order is not always obvious at a casual glance. Some seventy different grasses appear on the list for Padre Island National Seashore alone.

To classify or name the varied grasses does not capture the subtle beauty they impart. Bending to the breeze, they twist and turn in contorted yet graceful shapes, disappearing beneath the drifts and emerging unexpectedly in colorful accents like brush strokes on the artist's canvas of white sand. Windblown, they trace patterns on that canvas, delicate etchings that may well go unseen, soon to be erased and then retraced again.

Nor can the species list emphasize enough the importance of the grasses to the dunes and, still more vital, to the entire environment of the coast.

The foredunes are the guardians of the coast, barriers to storm-driven waves that hurl themselves upon the beach and batter at

the natural seawalls made of sand. Reinforced and stabilized by plants, the dunes rebuff the surging tides.

Should the mat of vegetation be destroyed or broached, however, the sand can no longer resist the persistent wind. Blowouts occur, with that sand being carried inland, adding to the lower sand flats and back-island dune fields. The dunes become increasingly active, moving and shifting and opening pathways for further erosion of their slopes.

Then storm tides penetrate the gaps in the defense and wash still more sand away. Waves lap across the barrier islands, perhaps even cutting new channels through which the tides can flow.

The fury of wind and water floods the marshes and bays and assaults the bay-front beaches, uprooting trees and smaller plants and driving animals before it from their low-lying homes. Chaos reigns for the duration of the siege.

Slowly the environment recovers from each such storm or major hurricane. New plants grow in place of old. Wildlife populations build and peak again, perhaps reaching even higher levels in new habitats created by the floods. Nature is amazingly resilient.

Even when no such fierce storm assaults the dunes, disruption of the vegetation by fire, drought, or man's destructiveness leads to obvious changes in the appearance of the coast.

Sand hills and flats that lie inland from the beach are fed by blowouts in the foredune ridge. Very little sand is transferred across a vegetation line, yet when such blowout dune fields are connected to the beach, sand is continually added to the active dunes that move northwestward with the winds.

Transverse and crescent-shaped barchan dunes, most of them less than ten feet high, are typical of the summer season, growing during the months of prevailing southeasterly winds that blow mainly from that single direction. Balmy breezes carry only the lightest grains of sand, tumbling and swirling aside the heavier particles to make transverse ridges across the direction of flow. When sand is in relatively short supply, the barchan dunes are

formed. The wind blows sand more readily over the low tips than over the higher central crest, and the crescent is convex toward the wind, with the tips pointing leeward.

Winter storms, in turn, modify these forms, for then the strongest winds come from the north. The "northers" pick up the sands shaped by summer and swirl them yet again, following still another blueprint for the architecture of the shifting dunes.

In this dynamic, constantly changing world, dune slopes form and are compressed before winds veer to change the angle of those slopes again. Perhaps someday, millions of years hence, the sands will have been turned to stone, the record of the winds preserved in cemented, cross-bedded planes as beautiful and bold as any sculpture yet displayed on earth.

Some of the same sand grains that now lie loose atop the dunes may once have been part of just such sandstone, a product of yet another beachside dune along some prehistoric sea. Eroded from their matrix, they have been recycled one more time.

However dynamic the dunes may be over a span of months and years, however fleeting they may be in terms of geologic time, they seem of the moment quiet and serene. A plume of sand may blow from the crest and the grasses bow to the wind, but there is little indication of the animal community that makes the sand its home. Beneath the broiling Texas sun the landscape appears almost devoid of life.

The clues are subtle at midday. A feather lies on the sand among the grasses, dropped by a gull in early molt. A line of tracks, mere dimples filling rapidly, leads from one clump of vegetation to another. Holes, half blocked by drifting sand, dot the slopes.

Just as each plant species has its own way of coping with the seemingly hostile terrain, so does each kind of animal. In many cases the methods are the same. They hide from the sun. They become nocturnal.

With the darkness, inhabitants of the dunes emerge from their burrows or from the shelter of a driftwood log or tangled vine. Grasshop-

Bird and ghost crab tracks

Lizard tracks

pers, katydids, and beetles crawl across the sand to feed on leaves and flowers that may themselves just be opening to the moon and stars. Lizards, their long toes splayed for traction, dart about in search of insect prey.

Ghost crabs, *Ocypode,* the great excavators of the upper beach and foredune ridge, leave their tunnels and descend to the surf to soak and exchange the seawater in their gill chambers. They are among the many scavengers of the beach, feeding on the casualties and leavings of the day.

Pocket gophers, whose mounds are abundant on the dunes and sandy soil inland, seldom leave the security of their burrows, instead feeding on roots and tubers and green plants pulled beneath the ground. Other rodents, however, emerge to forage for seeds, greens, and occasional insects.

During cloudy weather or in the cool of winter this activity may continue on into the day, but the heat of summer brings it to an early halt. Crabs and rodents retreat to their insulated burrows and seal them against the drying winds. Insects and reptiles seek the shade before the temperature of their cold-blooded bodies rises to lethal limits on the sand.

They leave behind a maze of tracks, each a chronicle of one creature's struggle for survival. Mouse, crab, bird, lizard, beetle—each venturer's trail holds a story that is written on the dune.

Surprises await the visitor to the dunes. Fragile mushrooms, anachronisms that would appear more at home in the leaf litter of a forest floor, spring from seemingly lifeless sand. Tiny red rosettes of sundews hug the ground amidst the dunes of Padre Island, their sticky leaves trapping hapless insects on which they feed. These carnivorous plants are more to be expected in the acid bogs of deep East Texas, yet here they find a similar environmental niche of nitrogen-poor soil and supply their need for that element with nutrients from the bodies of their prey.

Baby killdeer

During the breeding season of spring and summer, newly hatched baby birds scamper about on ridiculously large feet, hiding among the grasses or in shadowed depressions when approached. They, too, must seek shelter from countless enemies and the unrelenting sun.

Camouflage patterns serve to protect many of the dune inhabitants from the prying eyes of potential predators. The keeled earless lizard, common on the southern barrier islands, is nearly invisible against the backdrop of white sand. On cool days it basks in the warmth of the sun, secure in the instinctive knowledge that it will probably remain unseen. Only when this instinct gives way to fright and it darts across the sand does it appear to be more than a small portion of the landscape.

This lizard of the glistening sands, which gets its name from its lack of external ear openings, is lighter in color than its inland relatives, presumably an adaptation for defense. Such is the case with many species of the des-

Keeled earless lizard

erts and dunes; over the millennia they have grown paler to blend with their surroundings. Their chances for survival are thus greatly enhanced, and they will pass on the useful genetic trait to generations yet to come.

Other adaptations for a life spent among the drifting dunes are many and varied. Pocket mice and kangaroo rats manufacture within their bodies life-giving moisture from the seeds and occasional green plants on which they feed, thereby going indefinitely without drinking in this land where fresh water is in short supply. In nocturnal excursions from their burrows they gather food and transport it back to safety in fur-lined cheek pouches packed to overflowing. The large hind feet serve them well as they dash for their lives across the soft sands and dig with startling speed to vanish behind a crystal blizzard of flying grains.

While moles and pocket gophers remain beneath the sand, seldom emerging from their subterranean tunnel systems, a half-dozen bat species course the skies above, hunting insects on the wing. Few are permanent residents of this coastal zone, for they retreat to inland shelters when the first rays of dawn light the eastern sky.

Jackrabbits, skunks, weasels, badgers, and raccoons may all wander the coastal dunes from time to time, the big-eared jackrabbits feeding on succulent plants while the carnivores pursue more mobile meals. Coyotes, too, are frequent visitors, their presence revealed most often by fresh tracks or eerie choruses. They trot along the beach and prowl the dunes in dual roles of predator and scavenger, undiscriminating in their tastes in food.

Extremely efficient in its role as predator is the western diamondback rattlesnake. It is a large snake, sometimes reaching more than six feet in length, and it is relatively common on the coastal sands. The body coloration is sandy gray or brown with dark-edged diamonds down the back, and the tail is ringed with bands of alternating black and white. It

Western coachwhip

is surprisingly hard to see among the wave-driven debris scattered throughout the dunes.

Hunting by smell, by sight, and with the aid of heat-sensing devices possessed by it and other "pit vipers," the rattlesnake strikes with venomous hypodermic fangs. A careless rodent or rabbit pays the price, for that is the way the system works. It is a selective system that has assured the continued existence of both predator and prey.

Less formidable are several other snake species of the dunes. They too, however, have their predator roles to play. The hognose snake, master of the bluff, is relatively slow, relying on threat displays and camouflage to keep from being the hunted rather than the hunter. The coachwhip is long and slim, among the fastest of its kind, the serpentine body flowing with sinuous grace across the sand. With this speed and large, keen eyes it is a master hunter of rodents, small birds, lizards, and even other snakes.

Even fragile butterflies find sustenance and shelter in this seemingly hostile world of sand. Some are here because their larvae feed on plants adapted to the dunes. The caterpillars hatch from eggs, grow, pupate, and metamorphose into winged adults, sometimes on a single plant. This transformation is, without a doubt, one of the major miracles of nature.

Other species come to sip the nectar of fragrant blooms. Huge swallowtails and tiny, iridescent blues, the largest and smallest of the clan; pierids, the common white and yellow butterflies; exotic-looking buckeyes that seem so partial to sun-baked sand; little orange and brown skippers with their darting flight—all come to feed and to drink at damp patches in the sand. Each unrolls its tightly coiled soda-straw proboscis and drinks in the fluids it needs for life.

Although most are colorful on their dorsal surfaces, many butterflies wear camouflage below. The question mark, for one, is brilliant orange above; sitting with closed wings, it becomes a dead leaf, betrayed only by the small

Question mark butterfly

Willet

silver markings that are responsible for its name. The two surfaces of the thin wing membrane, covered with overlapping scales like shingles on a roof, can be completely different in both color and pattern.

The insect world has its predators as well. Many are, for their size, among the most ferocious hunters of them all. Dragonflies, from their breeding grounds in nearby ponds and marshes, patrol the dunes on crisp, transparent wings, often perching on blades of grass to gaze about with enormous compound eyes. Spotting a passing mosquito, midge, or fly, they dart out to catch it in the air and eat it ravenously with powerful cutting mandibles. The morsel will sate the burning hunger only for a moment.

Tiger beetles stalk their victims on the ground, running rapidly on long legs and seizing small insects in formidable sickle-shaped jaws. Common on the coastal dunes, they also frequent other sandy habitats across the continent. They are primarily diurnal crea-

tures, seeming to prefer the heat of the sun, and are frequently adorned with shiny metallic colors with a lovely iridescent sheen.

Most visible of the animals encountered on the dunes, perhaps, are the many species of birds. Because of their mobility, they are not restricted to a single habitat, but are free to range across the entire profile of the coast. Some are primarily birds of the open, sandy shores; others are more common in the adjoining marshes and mud flats. All may at times use the dunes for feeding grounds or nesting areas or simply as shelters from inclement weather or during long migration flights.

Mourning doves, savannah sparrows, and colorful horned larks forage for seeds of the grasses, crotons, composites, and other sandhill plants. Meadowlarks seek both seeds and insects and perch on the tops of the dunes to sing again and again their cheerful melodies. They are primarily eastern meadowlarks, but in winter a few of their western counterparts also wander to the coast, particularly in the southern portion of the state. Though similar in plumage, the latter can be distinguished by their more complex, flutelike song.

Scissor-tailed flycatchers, delicately beautiful with subtle colors and streaming tail feathers, hawk insects throughout the long summer days. At dusk, or beneath threatening storm clouds, they are replaced by long-winged nighthawks that wheel with incredible grace and power-dive in a whirring rush of air.

Tall, stately sandhill cranes stride across the sand, stopping to pick deliberately at seeds and roots or to capture occasional insects, crabs, lizards, snakes, and almost anything else small enough to swallow. Less famous than their larger white cousins, the endangered whooping cranes, these gray birds are nonetheless impressive in their own right, with wingspreads spanning nearly seven feet. They are most abundant on the coastal prairies and cultivated fields farther inland, where they winter in large flocks, but small groups are frequently to be encountered in the dunes.

Winter is also the season of the raptors, the birds of prey that descend along the coast to seek more abundant food supplies as chill winds sweep the North. American kestrels, formerly called sparrow hawks, hover on beating wings or perch on the highest vantage points to scan the sands with piercing eyes. Smallest of the falcons, they hunt insects, small reptiles, and careless rodents that might venture out by day.

Occasionally the slightly larger merlin and the strikingly handsome, moustachioed peregrine falcon range along the coast as well, feeding on small birds that cannot escape their blazing speed.

Marsh hawks sail low over the grasses, tilting and turning with the swirling breeze. Red-tailed hawks soar higher, broad wings and tail fanned to take advantage of the thermals rising from the sun-warmed sands. A lone silhouette atop a dune might prove to be a rare rough-legged or ferruginous hawk or a dozing short-eared owl waiting its turn to fly patrol. Each has its own specific niche to fill.

Many of the gulls, terns, and shorebirds that winter in tremendous flocks along the Gulf migrate northward for the summer, some venturing as far as the Arctic tundra to take advantage of the longer days and abundant food supply. Others, however, remain on the Texas coast to lay their eggs and raise their young. For these birds, the elevated dunes provide security from storm tides and rain-triggered flooding as well as from the more numerous predators that stalk the nearby marsh.

Some nest among the highest dunes, perhaps seeking partial shelter beneath an overhanging clump of grass or beside a massive driftwood log. Some choose the upper reaches of the beach, where storm-tossed shells lie bleaching in the drifting sand.

One of the most unusual and striking of the birds that nest along the Texas coast is the black skimmer, a distant relative of the gulls and terns. It is the only member of the skimmer family found in North America, although two others occur in other portions of the world. Black above and white below, the skimmer has a black-tipped, bright red bill that is unique in having a jutting lower mandible much longer than the upper one.

With this unusual beak, the skimmer captures small fish, shrimp, and other crustaceans that abound in the Gulf and quiet bays. Skimming the surface, the knife-edged mandible cutting a furrow through the water, it clamps down instantly on any aquatic creature with which it comes in contact. After making one pass, the skimmer often turns and retraces its path, thus catching other prey attracted to the disturbance of its wake.

The female black skimmer molds a shallow depression with her body and lays her spotted eggs directly on the sand, usually in a colony with others of her kind. She incubates the eggs alone, keeping them warm against a chill or sheltering them from the summer sun that can be just as deadly as the cold. The male frequently stands in attendance by her side.

Black skimmer and nest

Black skimmer family

The downy chicks, too, are brooded as protection from the elements or prowling enemies. Soon they are able to scamper about and seek shelter on their own until their parents return from fishing to feed them a portion of the catch.

When disturbed, the skimmers take to the air *en masse*, uttering strange yelping cries and swooping low to distract intruders. Such behavior is typical of the colonial gulls and terns as well and is sometimes carried to the point of physical attack with sharp-pointed beaks, all in defense of the precious eggs and young.

Mobbing behavior is but one of the instinctive means by which the birds protect their nests. Some merely steal silently away at the first sign of danger so as not to betray the site, trusting that the eggs will not be found. Other parents deliberately attempt to lead an intruder from the nest, perhaps trailing a "broken" wing and fluttering along with woeful cries. The instincts for survival are strong; the

behavioral devices, varied and fascinating.

Laughing gulls, common year-round residents and the only gulls that remain on the Texas coast to breed, also nest in colonies upon the ground. They might choose the low dune area of a barrier island or a sandy or grassy spot in a more protected bay. There they pull together plant stalks, grasses, and feathers to build their nests and lay three eggs marked cryptically with spots and scrawls.

Terns, too, share these breeding grounds. Caspian, royal, Sandwich, Forster's, gull-billed, and least terns all flock to nest along the coast. Forster's tern may make some effort to build a nest of grass and casual debris; the others simply use a depression in the sand.

Most shorebirds leave the South when spring arrives, but several species remain behind. Killdeer, Wilson's plovers, and American oystercatchers nest on barren sand or shell; willets more often seek the cover of a clump of grass.

Among these birds so intimately associated

Forster's tern and nest

Common nighthawk

Newly hatched least terns

with the shore are others of more cosmopolitan habits. The common nighthawk, for one, might lay its eggs on the ground at the edge of a pine forest, in an open field, or even on a flat city roof. A shell-covered dune is adequate as well. Not really a hawk at all, the nighthawk is a close relative of the whip-poor-will. To add to the confusion, the family is often called the "goatsuckers," another name dating back to folklore and long since shown to be fanciful.

All these species have proved effective in the reproductive race; all have arrived at much the same methods to insure perpetuation of their genes. In response to the stringent demands of the environment in which they live, the birds of beach and dunes have developed similar nesting traits.

Avian species elsewhere protect their progeny by placing nests in locations that are difficult for predators to reach. They might be in the tops of tall trees or in holes in their trunks, on rocky cliffs, or concealed among thick or spiny shrubs. These methods, obviously, are of little use on relatively empty sands. Other mechanisms have therefore evolved.

The central theme is camouflage of both the eggs and newborn young. The dunes are no place for eggs of gleaming white or colorful robin's-egg blue. Instead, the colors are shades of cream and buff and olive brown, ornamented with markings of darker hue. Lying directly on the sand or among the scattered, sun-dried grasses, they seem to vanish completely, another example of nature's sleight-of-hand.

Even within a single species, eggs vary greatly in both color and pattern. One Forster's tern might lay mottled brown eggs, while a neighboring nest holds greenish ones with chocolate spots. Eggs of royal terns range from nearly white to cream or pink; some are finely dotted, while others are heavily patterned with blotches or scrawls. Not only does the variation add to the effectiveness of the camouflage, but also it appears that some birds learn to recognize their own eggs by sight, a useful ability in a crowded colony.

One special instinct some species have for cooling both themselves and their eggs is called "belly soaking." Periodically the incubating bird leaves the nest and flies to the nearest water. There it wets its belly feathers and returns to stand above the nest to dry, acting as an evaporative cooler in the breeze.

The marvelous camouflage patterns that protect the eggs ordinarily extend to the young as well. Most babies of ground-nesting birds emerge already covered with downy feathers. Their eyes are open, and they can scamper about soon after they have rested and dried. Thus they are able to seek shelter and to hide from potential enemies. When they freeze motionless in the shadow of a leaf or shell, their cryptic patterns match the sand and make them almost impossible to find.

Such well-developed baby birds are called "precocial." Their counterparts in more sheltered nests are likely to be naked, blind, and helpless, a state referred to as "altricial." A hatchling robin can survive in such a helpless state, for it has the added protection of a warm, secure nest above the ground. A killdeer hatched at such a stage upon the sand could scarcely hope to make it through the day.

Because precocial birds are more fully developed when they hatch, they must spend a longer time within the egg. This necessitates more yolk for nourishment and thus, of course, a larger egg.

Although the adults are about the same size, the altricial robin hatches in twelve to fourteen days, while the incubation period for the precocial killdeer is nearly twice that long. The baby robin emerges quickly from its small egg and grows within the safety of the nest; the killdeer grows within its larger egg and emerges more prepared to face a hostile world.

Because of the large size of the eggs and the lack of a nest to confine them, most birds of the dunes have small clutch sizes. The royal tern lays but a single egg; the least tern, only two or three. Apparently this is the optimum number that can be sheltered beneath the body of the parent bird.

Most shorebirds—the sandpipers, plovers, and their relatives—lay four eggs. Seldom are there more or fewer. Sharply pointed at the smaller end, they fit nicely and compactly together like slices of a pie, enabling the adult to incubate them all.

The fascination of the dunes is boundless. The plants and animals that call them home cling to life with a tenacity beyond belief, adopting myriad means to cope with conditions most others could not endure. There is incomparable beauty in patterns traced by wind-blown grass and in the tracks of birds and ghost crabs on wave-surfaced sand. There is mystery here, and discovery, too. There is a sense of adventure and of challenge that leads one on.

The essence of the dunes is at once a feeling of barrenness and of bounty, a subtle hint of both stability and constant change. The sands shift and move and settle down again, perhaps to stay; but then, perhaps not. Waves attack the lower slopes, washing away the work of years, yet rebuilding will begin at once. Winds swirl and banners of crystal blow from high dune crests, yet the sand will soon be added to another hill.

Winter cold and summer heat both have their time, although the former seldom holds sway for long on this subtropic coast. More often it is the blazing sun that sets the tempo of the dunes. It is the sun that also determines the daily rhythm of life on the glistening sand. Some denizens of the dunes shrink from the light, emerging only under cover of darkness to search for food or mates or to satisfy whatever urge is greatest at the time. Night creatures are much more abundant than they seem.

With dawn's light those nocturnal inhabitants are gone, their places taken by others that prefer the day. Birds replace the bats and

Bird and ghost crab tracks

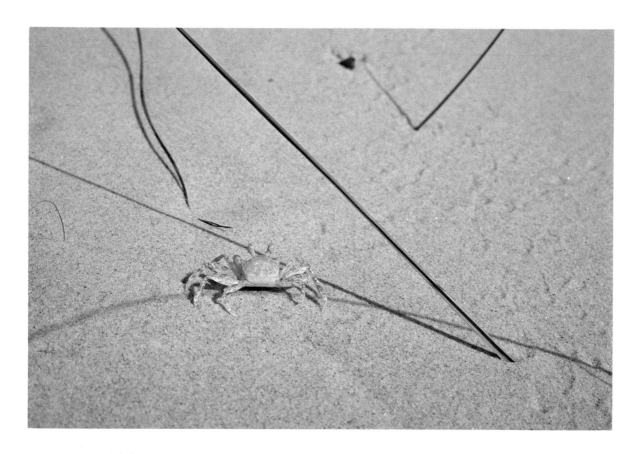

Ghost crab

Ghost crab

rodents, perhaps seeking much the same insect life or seeds to eat. Cold-blooded lizards, beetles, and butterflies bask in the sun if the night air has been cool at all, for they must raise their body temperatures in order to function at full speed.

Midday brings a quiet lull until the sun begins to drop and shadows stretch across the sand. Then the diurnal creatures hunt again, in one last flurry of activity before quitting for the night.

It is in this time of lengthening shadows that the dunes are at their best. It is then that the ripples and swirls of sifted sand become incomparable works of art. Colors washed out by a noontime sun reappear in bold brush strokes. A ghost crab walking on tiptoes across the textured sand is followed by a shadow of gargantuan proportions. It stops in wary watchfulness with keen eyes raised upon their stalks. Some flowers begin to open flaring petals to the night, while others close in tribute to the setting sun.

It is a magic time of day, a time that turns the sand to burnished gold, and the sea oats stand in silhouette against the darkening sky.

Sea oats

Bushy bluestem grass and live oaks

Broad expanses of marshland line the Texas coast, pockmarking the low-lying coastal plain. Along the northeastern portion, near the Louisiana border, the marshes extend virtually into the Gulf of Mexico. Farther down the curving coast they lie behind the beaches and dunes of the barrier islands, surrounding the many bays and extending farther inland along the river courses.

The marsh is not an easily defined entity, for there are many different types of habitats. Some are distinctly saline, inundated by the daily tides that flow across the bays and mud flats, even though normal tidal heights are no more than a foot or two.

Others, of course, are freshwater marshes, fed by the rivers and bayous that drain into the bays. They may also depend on an accumulation of rainwater, not only from the normal passage of fronts across the state but also from torrential downpours triggered by tropical storms and hurricanes. Because the topography is so flat and low, there is little drainage, and the water remains until it evaporates.

Between the two extremes are zones of brackish marsh, the salinity depending on the relative amounts of freshwater coming down the streams and saltwater from the tidal action. A period of heavy rains results in a great decrease in salinity, while high storm tides in times of drought have just the opposite effect.

Indeed, wind direction may play a greater role than the normal fluctuation of the tides. Southeasterly winds from the Gulf drive seawater up into the bays, producing unusually high tides; northwesterly winds that follow winter cold fronts quite literally blow the water from the bays. Tides in the latter case are then extremely low.

The salt marsh is most readily characterized by the kinds of plants that grow in it, for it supports a very specialized type of vegetation. Few of the plants that grow on higher ground could stand to have their roots constantly submerged and their foliage periodically

Marsh grasses and algae

Spiderwort

Salt-marsh morning-glory

bathed in salt solution. Trees can grow only on coastal ridges or salt domes where they are raised above the surrounding flood, although stands of low black mangroves populate some bays along the central coast.

The prominent floral feature of the salt marsh and bayshore is smooth cordgrass, *Spartina alterniflora*, a coarse grass that thrives in standing water and saturated, muddy soil. At a slightly higher elevation it is replaced by the related marshhay cordgrass, *Spartina patens*, a species that prefers a somewhat drier habitat. In damp, heavy soil it tends to grow in dense clumps, while a more slender, sparsely growing form occurs on the low dunes and sandy flats.

Most of the other salt-marsh plants are also grasses, but *Salicornia*, sea-purslane, seaside goldenrod, and others of the low-dune community will populate the outer fringes of the marsh. Algal forms are always present in the water, sometimes forming thick mats of brilliant green.

Freshwater marshes, on the other hand, provide a less demanding habitat, and consequently the variety of plant life is far greater there than in the saline ones. Although few trees are adapted to grow in standing water, several species can withstand short periods of flooding. Even the coastal live oaks thrive on small hummocks in the marshy ground.

Again, grasses tend to dominate the scene, one of the most distinctive being bushy bluestem, *Andropogon glomeratus*, with its fluffy, broomlike heads. A variety of sedges and rushes also occur.

More colorful wild flowers, too, dot the freshwater marsh, blooming throughout most of the year in a climate moderated by its proximity to the sea. Hundreds of species can be identified between the Sabine and the Rio Grande, some very local in their distribution and others more generally widespread. Some of the flowers are very large; some are barely noticeable among the tangled grasses on the ground. There is no standard formula, but the

Water-hyacinths

Katydid feeding on a blue water-lily

Crab spider with hairstreak butterfly

Praying mantis eating dragonfly

object is always the same: all must be pollinated to produce seeds. In some eyes, beauty may well be its own excuse for being, but the flowering plant has a more demanding task than simply providing beauty. Its very survival is at stake.

A few grow submerged in the shallow ponds, while others—cat-tails, iris, pickerelweed, arrowheads—stretch long stems and leaves above the surface of the water. Waterlilies, though rooted in the mud, send up floating leaves to manufacture food, and water-hyacinths drift freely with the wind until their combined mass has filled the empty space. Each has its own means to reach for the sun, just as the vining morning-glories and other climbers use their neighbors for support.

Here beneath the Texas sun the plants form a living tapestry of green, with different tints and shades and different textures to the leaves. Some are bright and glowing; others are subdued. There are lime greens of new growth, gray greens, shades of olive, and brilliant emerald hues. These are the only things on earth, these green and growing plants, that can manufacture their own food. With the energy of the sun and the catalysis of chlorophyll, they combine carbon dioxide and water into the sugars that provide them sustenance. Whatever shade of green the chlorophyll imparts, it is the vital link in the photosynthesis.

This conversion of solar energy into food is the center of life in the marsh, for it is on the plant life that all animals depend. Tiny snails graze upon the grasses and algal mats, while large deer browse on leaves or tender shoots. Mice and rabbits consume greens and seeds. Hundreds of species of caterpillars, grasshoppers, true bugs, and beetles feed voraciously, each preferring the particular plant forms that it has been programmed to seek out instinctively.

The plant eaters may then, in turn, be eaten by other animals, for most creatures are both hunters and hunted. Each is a link in one or more food chains. A plant produces leaves or flowers that are eaten by a caterpillar, and the caterpillar is then attacked by a predaceous wasp. Next, the wasp is caught in a spider's web. A frog then eats the spider, and a snake captures the frog. Finally, a hungry hawk devours the snake.

The chain may branch at any point, because most smaller animals, at least, face many different predators. There is intense competition for both plant and animal foods. The complex food chains form a network involving every creature in the marsh.

The network does not end at the borders of the salt- or freshwater marsh, of course, for some individuals interact with those from other habitats. Many are highly mobile and move from one zone to another. Aquatic species might range into the bays and open Gulf, while terrestrial species occasionally occupy the dunes or inland fields and forests. The result is an all-encompassing web of life. Early naturalist John Muir said it best: "When one tugs at a single thing in nature, he finds it attached to the rest of the world."

Predators employ many different methods to capture and subdue their prey. A few are venomous, while others rely on superior size or flashing speed. One of the most widespread tactics is that of disguise, and both the hunter and its quarry often resort to camouflage.

The praying mantis, in a cryptic pattern of green or grayish brown, sits undetected among the leaves, waiting for careless insects to wander within range. An ambush bug on a flower head looks like part of the plant until its spiny forelegs shoot out to grasp its prey. So, too, do snakes lie coiled patiently and frogs blend into the background beneath a tuft of grass. Although some spiders spin their sticky webs and others stalk relentlessly on foot, crab spiders wait in ambush on a matching flower. Any hungry bee or butterfly that happens by to dine may suddenly find itself being the dinner instead. The same animals that rely on deception to catch their prey derive protection from their camouflage as well, for something is certain to be stalking them in turn.

While most of the residents of the marsh are patterned to blend with their environment, some of the birds seem almost to flaunt

Little blue heron nest

Wilson's plover nest

their presence. That may, in fact, be their intention, for they establish territories and attract their mates by posturing display and song. They make up for their lack of discretion with alertness and ability to fly from danger.

It is during the nesting season that birds are especially subject to predation, particularly of the eggs and helpless young. Countless centuries of adaptation have provided several instinctive methods for protecting the nests, making use of the wide variety of vegetative habitats that occur within the marsh.

Many herons and their relatives choose to nest in colonies, building crude platforms of sticks in trees and shrubs. So strong is the communal response that there are frequently several nests in a single tree. The elevated sites offer protection from some predators, as do the combined clamor and the dagger-sharp beaks of the adults. Killdeer and Wilson's plovers select open places in which to lay their eggs directly on the ground. Like those of

Coot nest among blue water-lilies

Least bitterns

gulls and terns, the eggs are patterned so they are virtually impossible to find. Gallinules, coots, and grebes employ mounds of floating vegetation, and the common pied-billed grebe even goes to the extreme of covering its eggs each time it leaves the nest.

Typical of the many birds that nest among the dense grasses, rushes, and sedges of the marsh is the least bittern, the smallest of the heron family. The size of a meadowlark, it is not uncommon along the entire length of the Texas coast; however, it is so secretive that it is seldom seen. The bittern's nest is a platform of bent stalks just above the water; on the platform the female lays four or five white or pale blue eggs. Both sexes incubate, taking turns so that each is free to hunt for food. On the nest, the parent assumes the standard bittern pose, freezing motionless while peering out beneath the upthrust bill. With its subtle coloring and reed-thin silhouette, it blends perfectly into the marsh. If disturbed, it slips quietly away, striding rapidly through the

reeds by grasping the stems with its long toes and seldom flying unless closely approached.

Once the eggs hatch, the empty shells are discarded, presumably to help keep the nest clean and to prevent shiny shell fragments from revealing the location. The babies are partially covered with buffy down and are brooded against chill rains or scorching sun. They quickly adopt the protective pose and wait for meals of regurgitated fish, frogs, and crustaceans. Soon they, too, will be scrambling about in the marsh, climbing awkwardly at first with feet absurdly large for birds so young. Because both least bittern parents share the exacting domestic chores, both are protectively colored and display the secretive behavior.

The red-winged blackbird, one of the most abundant birds in North America and a resident of virtually every marsh, has a different style of life. Breeding males stake out their territories and guard them against other intruders. Disputes over territorial boundaries

Black-necked stilts

Fulvous harvest mice

are settled by stylized "fights" that involve exhibits of the brilliant crimson epaulets and shrill challenge songs of "konk-ka-ree."

When the females are ready to mate, they choose their nesting sites within the territory of a selected male. If the amorous attentions of a particular female are rejected, the male drives her off. If accepted, she joins his harem and begins to construct a woven nest of reeds and grass. The male takes no part in the building of the nest or in the incubation of the three to five blue green eggs marked with darker spots and scrawls. His function is one of territorial defense, and he loudly proclaims his dominion from the top of a bush or cattail stalk. The bright plumage of the male redwing is tailored for this task; the drab plumage of the female, for camouflage upon the nest.

Male and female black-necked stilts are almost identical in outward appearance, and neither is protectively colored. Instead, these lanky birds employ a different strategy, one of combined stealth and aggressive behavior. When they sense danger, they quietly slip from the nest and walk away, leaving the heavily patterned and beautifully camouflaged brown eggs in a bare scrape on the ground or in a crudely fashioned nest of dry grass and reeds. Once well away from the spot, they fly to the attack, hovering above the intruder and crying loudly in an attempt to distract it and lead it away. Only when the threat has passed do they return to the nest, one of them settling down over the eggs by awkwardly folding its long, ungainly legs.

Throughout the marsh are scores of other creatures that lay their eggs or give birth to live young in the relative safety of the dense vegetation. Mice of several species frequently live in underground burrows, but they may also place their nests at the base of sheltering clumps of grass or in bushes above the ground. Sometimes they appropriate abandoned bird nests as their own. The tiny baby

mice are born naked, blind, and helpless, but they grow very quickly and are ready to have young of their own by the time they are just a few months old.

Insects that are key links in the food chains of the marsh lay enormous numbers of eggs on the grasses and broad-leafed plants. Few of those eggs will survive through the stages of metamorphosis to become adults, but enough will escape predation and disease to provide for the continuation of the species.

Caterpillars of many kinds, the larvae of butterflies and moths, convert plants into food for carnivorous animals, including birds, small mammals, several reptiles and amphibians, spiders, and even other insects. In order to survive, they have evolved a number of defensive devices. Some have stinging spines, while others spin protective webs or hide behind amazing disguises and camouflage. Still others, like the monarch and queen that feed on milkweed, assimilate toxins from their food plants that make them poisonous to eat.

Queen butterfly on shore milkweed

Purple gallinule chick and blue water-lilies

Masked ducks

Such is also the case for species that consume leaves of the common passion-flower vine. Most of these caterpillars and their metamorphosed butterflies, instead of being camouflaged, are patterned brilliantly in orange or yellow, black, and white, warning colors in nature that mean, "Leave me alone." Many perfectly palatable species, however, mimic their toxic counterparts and undoubtedly derive some measure of protection from the charade.

Clearly the salt-, brackish-, and freshwater marshes teem with life of virtually every zoologic order. They are astonishingly rich environments, providing nutrients and shelter for large concentrations of inhabitants. Because they stretch along the entire coast, they offer, too, an avenue along which the more mobile animals can move, and so they function as interlocking channels for fish and other swimmers and as flyways for migratory birds.

It is during periods of high water after storms, for example, that rare birds may move northward from Mexico, following the flooded ponds and marshes like stepping stones on up the coast. Then the long-toed jacana, the "lily-trotter" of the tropics, can sometimes be seen, and the little masked duck may make a much heralded appearance, perhaps even to remain and rear a brood of young.

Though the insects, birds, and mammals are the most visible residents of the marsh, equally important are those that normally remain unseen beneath the surface of the water. Aquatic insects swim about or burrow in the bottom sediments, as do many kinds of worms and mollusks. Some crabs are found only in these shallows, sharing their muddy habitats with fish and shrimp. These creatures are the heartbeat of the marsh; without them there would be little else.

Many of the offshore inhabitants are likewise dependent on the saline and brackish marshes at some stage in their life. Young fish that hatch at sea are carried shoreward by the

Whooping crane

currents, and they enter the bays and estuaries, where they find greater protection among the grasses and reeds and profit from a more abundant food supply. Reaching maturity, perhaps after a year, they may then return to the Gulf to spawn.

Much the same cycle is observed by the commercial brown, pink, and white shrimp and by the blue crab. Spawning takes place offshore, and the larvae go through several free-swimming, planktonic stages. They then enter the bays and become bottom dwellers, remaining until nearly mature.

An estimated 90 percent of all the fish and shellfish harvested on the Texas coast depend on the estuaries for survival. An acre of brackish marsh can produce ten times as much protein as an acre of America's richest farmland. It is a lucrative and vital harvest.

Most famous of all the residents of the coastal marsh is probably the whooping crane. Standing nearly five feet tall, it is the

tallest bird in North America. Unfortunately, it is also one of the rarest.

Relics of the Pleistocene age, whooping cranes were apparently never numerous. They ranged, however, from the Arctic to Mexico and from Utah to South Carolina. Iowa was once a popular nesting ground for the big white birds with black wing tips and red faces, but as land cultivation increased, the shy and wary cranes declined.

A group that wintered in the Rio Grande Valley vanished in 1924, and a 1940 hurricane decimated a remnant nonmigratory flock in Louisiana. In 1941 the world's total population of whooping cranes, both wild and captive, hit a low of twenty-three birds. Fifteen of those wintered at Aransas National Wildlife Refuge, a 55,000-acre preserve established in 1937 to protect vanishing wildlife along Texas' central coast.

By 1948 the Louisiana cranes were gone forever, but the Aransas flock, with a total of thirty birds, was recovering slowly. There

Whooping cranes

have been several temporary setbacks, but in general the population has continued to climb, reaching seventy-eight in 1980 before inexplicably falling again to seventy-three in 1981. The cranes' future has become brighter over the last few years, but it is by no means assured.

The location of the whooping cranes' nesting ground was not known until 1954, in spite of an intensive search. Then a fire in Wood Buffalo National Park in Canada's Northwest Territories led to the discovery of the nests, and the mystery was solved. The almost impentrable maze of swampy ponds and heavy underbrush there offers the isolation the rare birds require, and protection by the governments of the United States and Canada will, it is hoped, assure their continued safety. The saga of the whooping crane has been described as "a love affair between a great white bird and two nations of people who have traditionally cheered for the underdog."

The female whooping crane lays two eggs,

but seldom does more than one survive. The adults frequently leave the nest when the first egg hatches, abandoning the other. If both eggs do hatch, the younger chick is unable to compete with its sibling. Discovery of this fact has led to an interesting experiment in which the "extra" eggs are removed and placed in the nests of sandhill cranes at Idaho's Grays Lake National Wildlife Refuge. The hatchlings then migrate with their foster parents to Bosque del Apache Refuge in New Mexico to spend the winter and return to Idaho each spring. Naturalists hope that a new and totally separate flock of whooping cranes can be established by this method, a flock far removed from any disaster that might threaten the Texas birds.

A week after hatching in Wood Buffalo Park, the young whooping cranes are able to follow their parents as they forage from pond to pond, and at the age of five months they make the 2,500-mile flight from Canada to the Texas coast, stopping often along the way

Great blue heron

Snowy egret

Snow goose

Barn owl

to rest and feed. Their rusty coloration is gradually lost through the winter season, and by the following summer the young cranes are in full adult plumage.

Upon arriving at Aransas in late autumn, each family group lays claim to a feeding territory of several hundred acres, which it jealously protects against all other cranes. Striding on long legs across the mud flats and tidal marshes, the parents and young feed voraciously on blue and fiddler crabs, crayfish, mud shrimp, frogs, and clams. Occasionally the diet is varied with such vegetable items as plant tubers, seeds and acorns.

Vast quantities of food are required by the cranes each day, part of the reason the family territories are so large. One female crane was observed picking up thirty-two clams, half of which she fed to her young, in thirty minutes. In one ten-minute interval a juvenile bird caught nine blue crabs and swallowed them whole. Obviously the estuaries must be very productive to support such feeding activity throughout the entire season, for the whoopers spend about three-fourths of the daylight hours feeding. The remainder of the day is spent resting, preening, or in territorial squabbles. The cranes roost at night standing in the water.

Frequently the families can be seen flying across the marsh on wings that span seven and one-half feet. Their trumpeting calls, for which they are named, can be heard for up to two miles.

As spring approaches, the cranes begin their spectacular courtship dances, bowing and leaping into the air with loud cries and flapping wings. Then, in late March or April, the family groups head north to the breeding grounds again. The young of the previous year will leave their parents upon reaching Canada, but the pairs are mated for life.

Surely the whooping cranes present one of nature's greatest wildlife spectacles and one that would be sorely missed if it were ever to vanish from the earth. It is a grave loss when any species passes into oblivion, never to be seen again, but the tragedy would seem somehow greater with a creature as magnificent as the whooping crane.

The same refuges that serve to protect such well-known species as those great white cranes are also, of course, beneficial to other rare forms of wildlife. Aransas also harbors the severely endangered Attwater's greater prairie chicken and osprey, peregrine falcon, bald eagle, and brown pelican. All are species that have been threatened with extinction.

Except for the prairie chicken, which is restricted to the upper portions of the coastal plain, these same endangered species might be seen at Laguna Atascosa National Wildlife Refuge in extreme South Texas. Established primarily for wintering waterfowl, Laguna Atascosa also provides habitat and protection for bird species found nowhere else in North America but in the Rio Grande Valley. Huge, noisy chachalacas strut through the underbrush, and colorful green jays and Altamira orioles perch in thorny trees and shrubs with such unfamiliar names as granjeno, retama, coyotillo, brasil, and Texas ebony. Here, too, are a few secretive ocelots, the lovely cats that have all but vanished north of the Rio Grande.

From the pot-holed cordgrass marshes near the Louisiana border to the Tamaulipan-scrub-bordered Laguna Madre, the four-hundred-mile Texas coast provides a winter home for hundreds of thousands of Canada, white-fronted, and snow geese, the latter occuring in both white and blue forms. The "blue goose," formerly regarded as a distinct species, has recently been discovered to be simply a color phase of the snow goose. The two freely interbreed, and goslings of both colors can emerge from the same clutch of eggs. Ironically, the common name remains "snow goose," while precedence dictates that the scientific name be *Chen caerulescens*, meaning "blue goose."

Nearly two dozen duck species inhabit the marshes and bays, most congregating in huge flocks during the winter months. There are coots, grebes, gallinules, and six species of the shy rails, including both yellow and black rails so seldom seen.

A dozen herons and egrets—together with the related white-faced and white ibises, wood stork, and roseate spoonbill—are found

Sharp-tailed sparrow

Great egret

Texas diamondback terrapin

Western cottonmouth

throughout the coastal region. The white egrets have recovered nicely from the persecution they suffered at the turn of the century, when they were shot by the boxcar load to provide feathers for ladies' hats.

Equally a part of the estuarial environment are those inhabitants with scaly skins. Alligators are the largest and most widely recognized—prehistoric relics that have survived almost unchanged from the era of the dinosaurs. They, too, were formerly on the list of endangered species because they were hunted for their valuable hides, but protection has recently restored them to the marsh. They are particularly abundant on the upper coast nearest the population center in Louisiana.

Unlike most other reptiles, the alligator exhibits a high degree of parental care, laying its eggs in a pile of grass and other vegetation and guarding them until they hatch. The young are about nine inches long at hatching and are marked with bright yellow crossbands on a dark background. The colorful

Baby American alligator

pattern is lost with age as the adults grow to a length of sixteen feet or more.

Snakes are common among the grasses and along the brushy edges of the bays and marshes. The western cottonmouth, or "water-moccasin," is not necessarily aggressive, but it will stand its ground in the face of an intruder and strike if threatened or provoked. While not likely to prove lethal, the venom causes severe pain and tissue damage. Like all seriously venomous North American snakes except the coral snake, the cottonmouth is a pit viper. Located between its eyes and nostrils are facial pits that act as infrared heat-sensing devices to help the snake detect warm-blooded prey.

A constant flicking of the tongue is a snake's way of investigating its surroundings, for the air samples it collects are analyzed by specialized organs within the head that provide a uniquely sensitive sense of smell. This is its principal contact with the world. Snakes are deaf to air-borne sounds, although they

Bullfrog

detect vibrations through the contact of their belly scales with the ground.

While venomous snakes are a very real part of almost any Texas marsh, most snakes are totally harmless to larger animals, including man. Far more common than the cottonmouth are innocuous water snakes of eight different species or subspecies, some of which can look quite ferocious in their bluff. Garter and ribbon snakes, the hognoses, rat snakes, racers, green snakes, the mud snake, and others all occur as well. Some grow to enormous size; others are so tiny that they are seldom noticed. All fit into the food chains that make up the web of life.

Mud turtles, snapping turtles, and several different sliders occupy the waters, while box turtles wander about the wooded edges of the marsh. The diamondback terrapin, however, inhabits only saltwater bays or brackish estuaries and does not venture into the freshwater systems that the other turtles seem to prefer. The terrapin has become quite rare in recent years and now is seldom seen.

Several frogs, ranging in size from giant bullfrogs to tiny cricket frogs scarcely more than an inch long, call throughout the spring and summer nights. Along with the toads and salamanders, they make up the amphibian portion of the marsh fauna, able to live at least a portion of their lives on land but returning to their ancestral homes in the water to lay their eggs.

Mammals are much more common than they first appear to be, but many are nocturnal and are seldom seen abroad in daylight. Others are shy and secretive, never venturing far from cover. Largest and best known is the white-tailed deer, a highly adaptable animal that occupies a wide range of habitats, from forests and fields to desert mountains and coastal marsh. A deer can slip through the long marsh grasses with surprising dexterity, blending into cover and disappearing like a wraith.

Raccoons, skunks, and minks are carnivores that prowl the marsh at night to satisfy a wide-ranging appetite. Otters swim the ponds and channels in search of the fish and crayfish that make up a major portion of their diet. Swamp rabbits are strictly herbivores, but these largest of the cottontails also swim of their own volition, something other rabbits are loath to do. Bats hunt the skies above the marsh, and tiny shrews hunt among the grasses, feeding an incessant and insatiable hunger that burns inside these smallest of mammals.

Most numerous of the mammals are the rodents, the rats and mice that reproduce at a furious rate and would quickly outstrip the food supply if they were not preyed upon by a wide assortment of other creatures. Snakes, hawks, owls, foxes, minks, skunks, and even shrews—all take large numbers of the harvest mice, rice rats, hispid cotton rats, and other species that abound in every corner of the marsh.

These rodents are not the same ones that have caused so many problems with destruction and disease around the world. They are, for the most part, harmless animals that have an important role to play. The problem species are the house mouse and the Norway and black rats, members of a different family than the native New World mice. They were unfortunately introduced into our environment and have proliferated out of control.

Another introduced species that has successfully established itself along the Gulf Coast is the nutria, often called the coypu. These large aquatic rodents, larger than the native muskrat, were brought to Louisiana from South America in 1938. Several escaped from their cages during a storm, and within five years they had spread throughout the southern portion of that state. It was not long at all before they had invaded Texas.

The nutria has become the most important fur-bearing mammal of the South in terms of trapping volume and revenue. It was hoped they would be useful in control of water-hyacinths and other troublesome weeds, but unfortunately they seem to prefer rice and sugarcane and raise havoc with dikes and irrigation systems with their burrowing.

The water-hyacinth that was brought from South America to a New Orleans cotton ex-

Nutria

White-tailed deer

American bittern

American bittern

position and given away as souvenirs; the starlings and house sparrows that were imported from Europe; the corbicula, or Asian clam, that is spreading through our waterways; fire ants, Japanese beetles, and gypsy moths; black mustard and Russian thistle—the roll of nuisance imports is impressive. It shows the delicate balance with which each thing is kept in check in its native habitat.

Unlike the others, one alien species now common on the Texas coast evidently arrived under its own power. Cattle egrets are immigrants from their native Africa and Eurasia, introduced first in South America and then on this continent, presumably borne on the winds of tropical storms. First seen in Texas in 1954, they nested five years later. Finding an ecological niche occupied by no other bird, they follow herds of cattle and feed on the insects chased up by them, much as they did in the wake of the vast game herds of the African plains. A census in 1976 indicated an amazing statewide population of 170,000 pairs, a number that has probably continued to grow. Although beneficial to man's interests in their feeding habits, it is possible that they may displace other herons from their limited nesting areas.

There is virtually no end to the list of interesting creatures to be encountered in the marsh. Here, in an array of different habitats, in the water and on the land, are plants and animals of every size and description. Each is adapted to its own way of life, but each is an integral part of the network that links all life together. Each, too, has a fascinating story to tell. Some stories are well-known, classic tales; some have yet to be read by anyone.

The marsh, of course, is not an isolated entity, nor is any other portion of our environment. Along the Texas coast the marsh is interlinked with the Gulf of Mexico, with bays and beaches and shifting dunes of glistening

sand. It is dependent on the rivers that flow from western highlands to the sea, and it is influenced by the forests and fields that surround it as it spreads its fingers inland along the fertile estuaries.

The beach, the dunes, the marsh—all are elements of a vital Texas coast. All are fascinating, and all are lovely, from sunrise on the Gulf to sunset in the marsh, and on into the night.

Photographer's Notes

It has not been an easy task to select the photographs for this book, for each is a labor of love. Although some were obtained almost by accident, others represent hours or days in a blind or miles of walking along the beach or through the marsh. The subjects have become friends, and it is hard to be objective.

Frontispiece. This long stretch of the Texas coast near Sabine was photographed from a helicopter at low altitude with a wide-angle lens. It represents the typical marshy land to be found along the upper coast.

Pages 16–17. Some photographs are carefully planned, but one of my favorite sunrises along the coast was, I admit, a matter of serendipity. Scheduled to make a peregrine falcon census along the beach from High Island to Sea Rim State Park, I arrived to discover that a storm tide blocked not only the beach but portions of the highway as well. Just then the sun came up in a blaze of color, and I scrambled frantically for my camera.

Pages 18–19. A sunrise trip to Galveston Island, on the other hand, was scheduled well in advance. Even though the clouds did not cooperate, the red sun through the haze and the play of light on the water made it worthwhile.

Page 20. Large flocks of gulls and terns often congregate along the beach. This flock at the Galveston jetty contained both royal and Forster's terns as well as ring-billed and laughing gulls, all in winter plumage. They were photographed with a 400-mm lens from the car, a convenient blind for such situations.

Page 21. Pelicans are delightful subjects. These were swimming around some shrimp boats, hoping for a handout.

Page 22. Watching two dowitchers through a 600-mm lens, I tried to catch them with bills submerged to show their feeding action. I suspect these are long-billed dowitchers, but it is difficult to tell them from the short-billed species without hearing them call.

It is hard to resist photographing the humorous-looking long-billed curlew. This one was walking on the beach at Rockport.

Pages 24–25. The willet is found everywhere along the Texas coast. This one was standing in a small pond on the beach at Galveston, and I sat quietly in my car and photographed it with a 400-mm lens at close range. I was pleased with the combination of bird, reflection, and shadow. The lifted wings show the flashy pattern that is hidden in repose.

Page 26. Waves leave an amazing variety of patterns in the sand. These two were photographed at Galveston.

Page 27. Foam on the beach has a wonderful iridescence in the sunlight.

Bird tracks form fascinating patterns in the soft sand. These tracks of gulls show the webbing between the toes.

Page 28. Hardly welcoming me with open arms, a blue crab assumes a defense posture as I approach. Its claws are capable of inflicting a painful nip.

After tipping its shell up to look inside, I had to lie in wait for several minutes before this shy hermit crab would venture out.

Page 29. Sea anemones exhibit a wide range of colors. These were attached to a Galveston rock groin and were partially covered with sand.

Page 30. Drifts of tiny shells often carpet sections of the beach. These little bivalves were photographed with a macro lens just as they were found near High Island. Many different species are represented.

Page 31. Most abundant of the large gastropods are the rock shells. With their wide range of colors and patterns, they form an attractive mosaic on the beach.

Pages 32–33. No two sunrises are ever quite the same. These, taken from different locations on the coast, were chosen for their wide range of colors and cloud effects.

Page 34. The laughing gull was stretching its wing when I photographed it with a 600-mm lens. From that distance I seemed to pose no threat, and the gull went through an elaborate routine that seemed almost choreographed.

Page 36. These male redheads were swimming near the beach at Rockport. Periodically they would rise in the water and flap their wings, an action I was able to capture with a 600-mm telephoto lens. The blurred wings provide the feeling of movement, while the head remains in sharp detail.

Page 37. The black-legged kittiwake is a rare winter straggler to the Texas coast from much farther north. This immature bird was present at the Texas City Dike for several days and proved to be an obliging model for a portrait.

Page 38. On a cool autumn morning, migrating monarch butterflies hang from a beachfront tamarisk where they spent the night. As the sun begins to warm their muscles, they spread their wings to absorb more of its energy. Some of these fragile insects will survive the winter in a hidden forest in Mexico.

From a driftwood log on the beach, tiny hatchling spiders disperse by spinning silken threads that catch the wind.

Page 39. Colonial tunicates coat a rock taken from the shallow water at South Padre Island. Here they are shown larger than life-size, the tiny individuals combining to form colonies of several different colors.

Captured larger than life with a macro lens, a tiny brittle star crawls upon the fingers of a sponge. This scene was photographed on South Padre Island, where such marine invertebrates are much more common than in the colder waters farther north.

Page 40. While most people are drawn to the beach in summer, I prefer to walk the sands on blustery winter days. The wind and surf then play an almost private concert, and the treasures of the sea lie washed up on the sand. On this day a squall moved up the coast near Galveston, and I remained to wander in the rain.

Page 41. Knots are uncommon winter birds along the Texas coast. These stand huddled against the chill wind and spray.

This laughing gull in immaculate spring plumage was photographed from the Galveston-Bolivar ferry as it followed in the wake. Using a short telephoto lens, I waited until the bird flew into focal range, its wings curving gracefully to cup the air. Somehow this flight seems to me the epitome of effortless grace and beauty.

Page 42. A Portuguese man-of-war washed up on the beach is artfully posed by the receding waves. These venomous invertebrates are sometimes present in large numbers on the coast.

Cabbagehead jellyfish are commonly seen along the beach, and I waited for a wave to add movement to the photograph.

Page 43. I found this southern stingray in shallow water along the beach of the Bolivar Peninsula. Carefully avoiding the spine on its tail, I waded in to take its picture.

On a stormy day in spring, the Galveston beach was covered with sargassum weed. Picking up great handfuls of it in the surf, I was able to find many of the sargassum animals, including this nudibranch, which was almost perfectly camouflaged in its algal home. Photographed with a macro lens, it is shown here half again life-size.

Page 44. This migrating monarch did not survive its southerly flight and lies upon a Galveston beach. Others, however, will fare better, and the species will survive.

While not, perhaps, a pretty sight, this dead sheepshead is also a part of the saga of the sea. The beach is the final resting place for many of the creatures that populate the waters of the Gulf of Mexico.

Page 45. Flying in a helicopter over the Gulf of Mexico, I photographed this rainbow that appeared near a thunderstorm. To my amazement, I saw rainbows that seemed to form full circles, dropping down to lie on the surface of the water and then rising in a full 360-degree arc.

Page 46. Near Sea Rim State Park, a pleistocene horse tooth lies washed up on the beach. Such fossils erode from a layer of Beaumont clay offshore and are relatively common along the upper reaches of the coast.

Page 47. A full moon casts a ghostly glow on scudding clouds and waves lapping on the beach. This photograph, taken at Padre Island National Seashore, required a time exposure of several seconds.

Pages 48–49, 50, 51. The sand dunes of Padre Island are the tallest and most beautiful of those along the Texas coast. Camping there for several days in my quest for pictures, I had this one perfect afternoon of blue skies and sunlit sand. The remainder of the time I was plagued by strong winds and, finally, by torrential rains that made photography all but impossible.

Pages 52–53. Wind patterns like these photographed on Mustang Island add almost infinite variety to the dunes. Low-angle light of early morning or late afternoon is best for capturing the textures of the sand.

Page 54. On Galveston Island, in the small dune field near the jetty, beach morning-glory anchors the sand in place. Below the vines, the unstable sand is in constant motion with the wind.

Page 55. This small dune on Padre Island is thickly covered with sunflowers and grasses.

Page 56. Both goat's-foot (*top*) and beach morning-glories are commonly found along much of the Texas coast. True to their name, they are best photographed before the sun shrivels the delicate blooms.

Page 57. Beach evening-primrose has delicate, large-petaled flowers, while those of sea-purslane are thick and tough. Both, however, were photographed on the sands of Galveston Island State Park.

The downy sunflower is a common species of the southern dunes, but this was a rare plant in which each composite flower head contained extra ray flowers, giving it a "double-flowered" appearance. It was photographed near Rockport.

Page 58. The remnant live oaks of Padre Island present a classic example of wind-shaped trees. They are all that remain of what was once a larger grove.

Page 59. Small details of the dunes are as fascinating as the whole. These grasses, on Galveston Island, somehow epitomize the struggle for survival in the blowing sand. It is amazing to me that something with such apparently fragile beauty can endure in the hostile environment.

Page 60. This expanse of rippling sand, accented by the grasses, was photographed on Mustang Island.

Page 62. A single feather among the grasses seemed to represent both the abundant life and the struggle for survival in the dunes.

Page 63. In early morning the sands of Padre Island are patterned with tracks of many different animals. It is always fun to seek them out and read the stories they contain.

Page 64. This newly hatched killdeer was found scampering about on the sands of Galveston Island. When approached too closely, he darted off on wobbly legs, but not before I photographed him with a macro lens.

Somehow a mushroom seems out of place on a sand dune. They are not uncommon, however, along much of the coast.

Page 65. The keeled earless lizard is a perfect example of camouflage. This one was photographed at night on Padre Island by means of a macro lens and a ring flash.

Page 66. Although few people admire snakes, they are an important part of the environment. Most, like this young coachwhip, are completely harmless to humans.

Page 67. Butterflies are as difficult to photograph as large animals, for their wary nature seldom allows close approach. This one, however, was so intent on drinking from a damp patch of sand that it let me crawl within inches with my close-up lens. The uncoiled tongue can be seen probing in the sand. Note also the different patterns on the ventral and dorsal surfaces and the silver mark that gives this question mark butterfly its name.

Page 68. A willet peers over a sand dune at the camera. It evidently had a nest nearby, but I was unable to locate it.

Page 70–71. From a blind set twenty feet away, I watch a black skimmer at its nest in the dunes of Galveston Island. Certainly this is one of the most striking of all our coastal birds.

On an island in Galveston Bay, a pair of black skimmers shelter their chick and unhatched egg from the blazing summer sun. Alert to the presence of the photographer, they utter loud cries of alarm.

Page 72. A Forster's tern incubates its eggs in a makeshift nest of grasses and feathers on the sand. Bill open and feathers ruffled, it pants in the summer heat. While these eggs were olive brown, those in an adjacent nest of the same species were bluish green.

Page 73. A nighthawk's eggs are beautifully camouflaged upon the sand, as is the bird itself with its cryptic plumage. This one had selected an island in Galveston Bay on which to nest.

Page 74. Two least terns lie huddled on the sand, one having just emerged from the egg. The egg tooth is visible as a white spot on its bill. These precocial birds are able to seek shelter soon after hatching, and their camouflaging downy feathers are a nearly perfect match for the surrounding sand.

Page 76. Swirling in the wind, grasses trace patterns of intricate beauty on a Padre Island dune.

Page 77. Birds and ghost crabs leave their tracks on a Padre Island dune.

Pages 78–79. Ghost crabs are delightful subjects for the photographer. Even though primarily nocturnal, some can generally be found during the day. By slow approach on hands and knees, I was able to shoot these pictures with a macro lens at close range.

Page 80. Sunset in the dunes is a very special time of day. The sand takes on the rich hues of the glowing sky, and the low angle of the light reveals every ripple. Such was the case after a perfect day on Padre Island.

Page 81. Sea oats on a dune top stand silhouetted against a Texas sunset.

Page 82–83. In mid-afternoon I discovered this marshy pond at Aransas National Wildlife Refuge. Hoping for a photogenic sunset, I waited several hours. I was not disappointed. This picture was taken with a 28-mm wide-angle lens, for the color spread across most of the western sky.

Page 84. Flying in a helicopter above the coastal marsh near Sabine, I took this picture with a wide-angle lens. It was not difficult to see what a haven for wildlife this area can be.

Pages 85–86. The freshwater marshes of Aransas Refuge contain hummocks on which live oaks grow. This blend of water, grass, and trees provides habitat for an enormous variety of wildlife.

Page 87. Here the sun beats down on a saline marsh at Sea Rim State Park, giving life to grasses and algae that will in turn serve as food for many creatures.

Page 88. Spiderworts and salt-marsh morning-glories are but two of the myriad wildflowers that bloom throughout the marsh.

Page 89. The imported water-hyacinth has become a nuisance plant, clogging waterways with its rapid, almost uncontrollable growth. Few plants, however, are any more beautiful than this one with its shiny green leaves and orchid flowers.

Page 90. Wading into a pond near Rockport to photograph a blue water-lily, I discovered a green katydid eating away at the flower. This is the first step in a food chain that might eventually involve many different animals.

At first I thought this hairstreak butterfly was sipping nectar from the flower; then I discovered it was instead caught in the clutches of a crab spider. The tableau was photographed with a macro lens and flash.

As I crept close to this praying mantis with camera and flash, he turned his head and looked at me. After several minutes he resumed eating the dragonfly. One voracious insect predator had succumbed to another.

Page 92. A little blue heron nest is little more than a crude platform of sticks, this one on an island in Galveston Bay. Herons of several species share the colony and compete for the nest sites in low trees and bushes.

Camouflage is the sole defense for these Wilson's plover eggs laid on the sand.

Page 93. This coot's nest was on a pile of floating reeds in an Anahuac pond. On three separate occasions I watched the bird bring fresh flowers and weave them into the nest, providing one of the most photogenic nests I have ever seen.

Page 94–95. For a period of five weeks I watched this family of least bitterns in a pond at Anahuac National Wildlife Refuge. From a blind fifteen feet away I saw the ritual greetings at the nest as the birds entwined their necks and rubbed their bills, and I watched as both male and female took turns incubating the four white eggs.

One day, through the small window of the blind, I saw the female pick up an empty egg shell and throw it out of the nest, the baby having just emerged. Instinctively I snapped the shutter without looking through the lens, and fortunately the tripod-mounted camera was properly set.

Within a day or two the babies had adopted the typical bittern pose, freezing motionless with bills pointed upward to blend with the reeds. In two weeks they were clambering about in the marsh, and they then disappeared from the nest site.

Page 96. Photographing a black-necked stilt from a blind, I noticed its mate approach the nest. As the two prepared to change places, their long legs seemed to get hopelessly in the way. I was able to snap a single picture of the comic-opera scene before they got untangled.

Rodents are perhaps the most numerous mammals of the marsh, yet their nocturnal habits keep them from being seen by the casual observer. This fulvous harvest mouse is very protective of her newborn babies.

Page 97. Looking for caterpillars in the marsh near Wallisville, Texas, I discovered a larva of the queen butterfly, a tropical relative of the monarch. It soon pupated on its milkweed foodplant, and a week later the butterfly emerged to spread its wings and fly away. This series was photographed with a macro lens and ring flash.

Page 98. A marsh overgrown with water-lilies provides a rich environment for many different plants and animals. Here, a newly hatched purple gallinule, white egg tooth still on its bill, tries its legs on a lily pad.

Page 99. One of the rarest birds to visit the Texas coast is the little masked duck, a species seldom photographed in color anywhere in the wild. This adult shepherds its brood through a marsh at Anahuac National Wildlife Refuge.

Page 100–101. No story of the Texas coast is complete without the whooping crane. After several trips into the waters of Aransas Refuge aboard Captain Brownie Brown's *Whooping Crane*, I was finally able to get some pictures of Texas' most famous birds. While this is sometimes an easy task, I was usually unlucky, suffering bad weather and uncooperative cranes. On the day they chose to wander within range of my 600-mm lens I was ecstatic.

Page 102. The wind-blown blue heron, stalking snowy egret, and shy snow goose were all photographed with a telephoto lens from a blind. The barn owl, on the other hand, was discovered asleep beneath a bush and photographed at close range with a normal lens before it flew away. Such are the vagaries of bird photography, a sport that is rapidly growing in popularity. Texas beaches and marshes attract many different kinds of birds, and there is no better place to start.

Page 104. This little sharp-tailed sparrow popped out of the grass in response to a squeaking noise I made, and I photographed it with a 600-mm lens.

Page 105. A short telephoto lens produced this picture of a great egret stalking through an Aransas marsh.

Page 106. Diamondback terrapins have become all too rare along the Texas coast. This one was found in a marsh on Galveston Island.

Angered by the presence of the photographer and ready to strike, a western cottonmouth is a formidable snake.

Page 107. A baby alligator, no more than a few weeks old, is brightly marked with yellow bands. Its tiny teeth are sharp but ineffectual against all but the smallest prey. Fortunately, with protection, the once endangered alligators are returning in good numbers.

A bullfrog on a lily pad seems almost a symbol of the southern marsh.

Page 109. Nestled in the grass beside an Anahuac Refuge pond, a nutria dozes in the afternoon sun. The photograph was taken with a 400-mm lens.

I have photographed white-tailed deer on many occasions, but this telephoto picture seemed to best capture the elusiveness of the handsome animals as they blend silently into the marsh grass of the Aransas Refuge.

Page 110–111. To me, the American bittern is the archetypical bird of the marsh. Perfectly camouflaged, it poses motionless to take advantage of its reedlike markings.

Page 112. The glow of sunset is mirrored in an Aransas pond.

Page 113. The sun sets on a colony of herons and egrets in Galveston Bay. This was the last photograph of the day on a trip with Texas Parks and Wildlife biologists to band these colonial water birds.